THE APPLAUSE ACTING SERIES

RECYCLING SHAKESPEARE

The Applause Acting Series

ACTING IN FILM by Michael Caine

ACTING IN RESTORATION COMEDY by Simon Callow

DIRECTING THE ACTION by Charles Marowitz

DUO! *The Best Scenes for the 90s*

THE MONOLOGUE WORKSHOP by Jack Poggi

ON SINGING ONSTAGE by David Craig

SHAKESCENES: *Shakespeare for Two*
    Edited by John Russell Brown

SOLILOQUY! *The Shakespeare Monologues (Men)*

SOLILOQUY! *The Shakespeare Monologues (Women)*

SOLO! *The Best Monologues of the 80s (Men)*

SOLO! *The Best Monologues of the 80s (Women)*

SPEAK WITH DISTINCTION by Edith Skinner
    Edited by Lilene Mansell and Timothy Monich
    90-minute audiocassette also available

THE STANISLAVSKY TECHNIQUE: RUSSIA
    A Workbook for Actors by Mel Gordon

Additional titles in preparation. Write to Applause Theatre Books
for further information and a catalog.

RECYCLING SHAKESPEARE

by Charles Marowitz

APPLAUSE
THEATRE BOOK PUBLISHERS
211 WEST 71 STREET • NEW YORK NY • 10023

RECYCLING SHAKESPEARE

Library of Congress Cataloging-in-Publication Data
Marowitz, Charles.
    Recycling Shakespeare / Charles Marowitz.
       p.   cm.—(The Dramatic medium)
    Includes bibliographical references and index.
    ISBN 1–55783–093–2: $32.95.—ISBN 1–55783–094–0 (pbk.): $14.95
    1. Shakespeare, William, 1564–1616—Criticism and interpretation
—History.   2. Shakespeare, William, 1564–1616—Stage history.
I. Title.   II. Series.
PR2965.M35   1991
822.3'3—dc20   90–22002
                                                                 CIP

Applause Theatre Book Publishers
211 West 71st Street
New York, NY 10023
(212) 595-4735

First Applause Printing, 1991

For Peter Brook
who first made me aware of the
buried treasure

And Jan Kott
who drew the map that led me to it

Contents

General editor's preface

The aim of the series is to analyse and redefine the nature of the dramatic medium. The work of structuralists and semiologists in recent years has considerably altered the implication of the term 'text' in the area of theatre studies. But in considering works in performance as well as the interrelationship of the contrasted elements of the medium an extension of this approach is demanded.

By examining the dramatic aspects of film, ballet and music-theatre along with the work of pioneer twentieth-century prac-titioners, the series aims to promote a richer understanding of the features and potential of theatrical language.

Basic to the series is an examination of the relationship between new developments in Europe and America, apparent in all areas of drama, from music-theatre and dance through to modern conventions of acting and directing.

David Hirst

Preface

This book is directed at two enemies – the academics and the traditionalists. Often they can be found together in an unholy alliance and, where they are, the works of Shakespeare are embalmed or rigidified, diminished or despoiled.

The assumption behind the book is that 'Shakespeare' is matter and matter can be reduced, expanded, transformed or reconstituted. To those who believe that 'a classic' is an entity fixed in time and bounded by text, this may be a rough ride.

Throughout the book, despite a tone which may seem arrogant and arbitrary, I am propounding views which are personal to myself and which I do not for a moment expect others to adopt. I am not proselytising 'a view of Shakespeare' with an eye towards effecting conversions. Unlike the views of scholars or critics, mine have evolved from hands-on experiences with several of Shakespeare's plays and it was not until reflecting on these experiences that I found I held these opinions.

In some ways, one's view of Shakepeare is analagous to one's view of art in general. The way in which one experiences a Shakespearian play is related to the way in which one comprehends life. Some people contend that Shakespearian truth is there to be discovered using the tools of the scholar, the critic and the historian. I would contend that Shakespeare is like a prism in which I discern innumerable reflections of myself and my society and, like a prism, it refracts many pinpoints of colour, rather than transmitting one unbroken light.

What I love best in Shakespeare are the facets of myself and my world that I find there. What I like least are the 'commercials' he has inspired over four centuries. What I abominate are the friends he has made over the past one hundred years. I have yet to reconcile myself to the paradox that I can love the work of a writer whose champions and stalwarts are so detestable.

Charles Marowitz

Note: The photograph on the front of the cover/jacket was taken by Ian Dryden. Every effort was made to contact the copyright-holder, without success; the publishers will be pleased to make the necessary arrangement at the first opportunity.

Harlotry in

1   b<u>ardo</u>latry

....

No one can deny the fact that a good deal of 'harlotry' has insinuated itself into bardolatry. When you have a large, multinational corporation such as the Shakespeare Industry, it goes without saying that it attracts people of easy virtue, and that's a subject I intend to return to.

As to my credentials, or my lack of them, I have to say that I argue from the view point of a professional director – not that of a scholar or a pedagogue. A director's relationship to Shakespearian scholarship (Granville-Barker notwithstanding) is very different from an academic's. For the academic, theories, suppositions and speculations are ends in themselves, and a really solid piece of Shakespearian criticism need only be well argued and well written to join the voluminous tomes of its predecessors. But a director is looking for what in the theatre are called 'playable values' – that is, ideas capable of being translated into concrete dramatic terms. Very often, scholars provide just that, and there is more 'scholarship' on view in classical productions throughout Europe and America than audiences tend to realise. Most directors prefer to play down the fact that many an original theatrical insight can be traced back, not to a director's leap-of-the-imagination, but to a scholar's dry-as-dust thesis. Three notable and acknowledged lifts immediately spring to mind: Laurence Olivier's Oedipal production of *Hamlet* in 1937, based on a psychoanalytical tract by Ernest Jones (*Hamlet and Oedipus*, 1949), Peter Brook's *King Lear* (1962), and The National Theatre's all-male *As You Like It* directed by Clifford Williams in 1969 – both derived in large part from essays in Jan Kott's *Shakespeare Our Contemporary* (1965).

'Playable values' are not always consistent with literary values. A scholarly insight can make very good sense and be untranslatable in stage terms. Conversely, a playable value can be

1

brilliantly effective in a *mise-en-scène* and yet not stand up to intellectual scrutiny after the event. A classic in production makes demands that are never called for in the study. And perhaps that is where so much of the trouble stems from. And by 'trouble' I mean the traditional animosity that tends to smoulder between the professional theatre and the academic community. There is a factor in Shakespearian production which never enters into the academic study of a text. It is a stubborn factor and a transforming factor and, unfortunately, one that will not go away. I refer of course to the director.

In the nineteenth century, men such as the Duke of Saxe-Meiningen, Henry Irving, and Herbert Beerbohm Tree were closer to chairmen-of-committees than what we, today, call modern directors. They supervised their actors and decided questions of design but they did not really insinuate a highly personal viewpoint into their productions. With the advent of Konstantin Stanislavsky in Russia, Augustin Daly in New York, and Max Reinhardt in Germany, the director, armed with a stylistic prerogative and an aesthetic bias, gradually came to the fore. In the 1920s and 1930s in France, with men such as Jacques Copeau, Charles Dullin, Gaston Baty, Louis Jouvet and Jean-Louis Barrault, and in Russia with Nikolai Evreinov, Eugene Vakhtangov and Vsevolod Meyerhold, we begin to see the first signs of another kind of director: men who leave their mark on material as much as they do on actors; directors who begin to reveal an attitude to new and established plays which is more pronounced than before. Sometimes, aggressively so.

The emergence of what we would call the modern director coincides not with his imposed authority on the physical elements of production, but his intercession with a playwright's ideas. The old autocrat–director controlled his actors; the modern director appropriates to himself those intellectual ingredients usually reserved for the playwright – using the tangible instruments of the stage as a kind of penmanship with which he alters or gives personal connotation to the text of writers both living and dead.

This is most visible in the works of Shakespeare and with directors such a Max Reinhardt, Benno Besson, Giorgio Strehler, Peter Stein and Peter Brook: men who began to produce resonances in established works which surprised audiences that never imagined the plays dealt with the themes they now seemed to be about. So that, for instance, there comes a production of *King Lear* which charts the rise of the bourgeoisie and the gradual disintegration of feudalism, or another which treats the play as an oriental fable entirely detached from any historical milieu, or a version in which it's seen as a bleak, apocalyptic vision unfolding in an arid, Beckettian landscape from which God has been banished.

In these instances, and in many others like them, what has changed is the philosophical framework in which the play was originally conceived: the 'spirit' of the work radically re-routed even though the 'letter' remains intact. In short another 'author' has appeared, and he is saying things different from – sometimes at conflict with – the meanings of the first author, and this inter-loper is, of course, the modern director; a man who insists on reading his own thoughts into those traditionally associated with the author whose work he is communicating.

A director who does not proceed in this way, who chains himself to unwavering fidelity to the author and pursues his work in selfless devotion to the 'meaning of the text' is unknowingly abdicating a director's responsibility. Since the only way to express an author's meaning is to filter it through the sensibility of those artists charged with communicating it, 'fidelity' is really a high-sounding word for 'lack of imaginative output'. The director who is committed to putting the play on the stage exactly as it is written is the equivalent of the cook who intends to make the omelette without cracking the eggs. The modern director is the master of the subtext as surely as the author is of the text, and his dominion includes every nuance and allusion transmitted in each moment of the performance. He is not simply a person who imposes order upon artistic subordinates in order to express a writer's meaning, but someone who challenges the assumptions of a work of art and uses *mise-en-scène* actively to pit his beliefs against those of the play. Without that confrontation, that sense of challenge, true direction cannot take place, for unless the author's work is engaged on an intellectual level equal to his own, the play is merely transplanted from one medium to another – a process which contradicts the definition of the word 'perform' – which means to 'carry on to the finish', to 'accomplish', to fulfil the cycle of creativity begun by the author.

Having cleared that deck, one can finally get to the subject. The great Shakespearian pastime has always been tendency-spotting – the intellectual equivalent of bird-watching – and anyone who has been hard at it has discovered the tendency, for example, towards bigger and more elaborate stage-settings;

toward politicising the histories; towards sexualising the mixed-gender comedies, etc., etc. But the tendency that interests me most is the separation that has begun to take place between the original plays and works on which they are loosely – sometimes remotely – based. To explain this tendency, I think it is useful to look at the recent TV adaptations of the collected works produced by the BBC.

The great lesson of those filmed Shakespearian plays is that, through the refusal to allow the material to transform – to adapt itself to a different medium – most of the works were denatured. One could praise this performance or that scenic idea, but, all in all, it produced leaden and inert television viewing. And why? Because the underlying assumption of the exercise was: the plays are so great, all one need do is bring together the best British talent one can find and record them for posterity. It is this high-varnish approach to Shakespeare which is his chiefest foe – the detestable conservative notion that all one ever needs do with 'classics' is preserve them.

One ought to be clear about this: the bastions that protect William Shakespeare have been established by scholars, critics and teachers – people with a vested interest in language and the furtherance of a literary tradition. It is in their interests that the texts remain sacrosanct, that they are handed down from generation to generation, each providing new insights and new refinements, like so many new glosses on an old painting. A process which, judging from the past two hundred years, can go on for at least another five hundred, because there will never be a shortage of scholars to point out the semiotic significance of the ass's head in *A Midsummer Night's Dream* or the tallow candle in *Macbeth* or the implications of the syllabus at Wittenberg during the years Hamlet was enrolled there.

In Academe it is considered a step up the ladder to be published in learned journals. It is a help in securing tenure and a fillip towards career advancement. Consequently the motive for publication is very much like a showcase production for an ambitious actor; a way of strutting his stuff – often at the expense of the material for which that 'stuff' is being 'strutted'. There is very little compulsion behind this kind of Shakespearian scholarship other than scoring points or sticking feathers in one's cap. Often the writer's underlying aim is merely to catch the attention of a department head or a fund-granting agency: what you might call 'harlotry' in 'bardolatry'. This accounts for the bizarre nature of many of those precious and far-fetched subjects. Then, of course, there is also that peculiar breed of niggling intellectual which actually enjoys picking at the chicken-bones of art in order to re-create a semblance of the whole bird. This breed accounts for many of those microscopic studies of Shakespearian works which seem to be obsessed with every grain, every wart, every follicle to be found in the collected works. They produce the papers that scrutinise the punctuation, the typography, the syntax and the topical allusions of every play. Not only do they not see the forests for the trees, they are often too fascinated by the sap on the bark even to see the trunk.

But for people without such obsessions, whose main concern is reconstituting Shakespeare's ideas and finding new ways drama-tically to extrapolate them, this myopic preoccupation with the canon seems, more than anything else, like the scrutiny of one chimpanzee fastidiously picking the nits off another.

Had the BBC treated the plays as 'material' to be refashioned for a new medium, had they not felt obliged to freeze them for posterity, each one might have been a unique televisual experi-ence, without losing the essence of the stage-work on which it was based: a method more successfully practised in motion pictures.

If you do a swift comparison of the early Shakespearian films with the later ones, you find that the biggest single difference is that in the 1930s there was a valiant attempt to stick to the narrative and, as much as possible, to the text, and these are virtually unwatchable today. But from the 1940s onward, film makers were more inclined to abandon the original texts and move off into purely cinematic directions. Which is why, for instance, Olivier's *Richard III* is so much better than Holly-wood's *As You Like It* with Elizabeth Bergner, directed by her husband Paul Czinner, or *Romeo and Juliet* starring a somewhat superannuated Norma Shearer and Leslie Howard. In *Richard III*, Olivier truncated the text, decided on three or four main character-points, and then expanded the battle scenes with a kind of inspired, epic film-making: the same scenes which on the stage usually consist of perfunctorily choreographed duels which almost always stop dead the action of the play. In Kenneth Branagh's 1989 remake, taking an almost opposite route, the film-maker explored the same material almost as a coming-of-age movie. What Shakespearian film-makers discovered was that the more one expanded the cinematic possibilities and the less one felt restricted by the strait-jacket of the text, the better the work was realised.

What is it for instance, about Kurosawa's *Ran*, that Japanese director's treatment of *King Lear*, which makes it a reinterpretation of Shakespeare's play and, at the same time, a bold diversion into a completely new work of art? For me, it is the liberty that Kurosawa exercises in following the play wherever, in his own personal imagination, it leads him. And if the imagination of an artist is rich and resourceful, it leads him to a highly personalised statement on the play's themes which could never have been made without taking the play as its point of departure.

Writing about this film, Jan Kott says:

> Kurosawa's greatness lies in his capacity to reveal a historical similarity and variance: to find a Shakespearian sense of doom in the other, remote, and apparently alien historical place. He trims the plot to the bone. Hidetora's three sons are all that remains of Lear's daughters and Gloucester's two sons. Shakespeare added the second plot of Gloucester, Edgar, and Edmund to the old folk tale about three daughters (two vile and one noble). Kurosawa has cut and compressed it. In this Japanese condensation of plot and character, only the eldest son's wife, a substitute for Goneril and Regan, is left in the castle where Hidetora has murdered her entire family. In this samurai epic, it is her drive for vengeance that destroys Hidetora's clan and legacy. (Jan Kott, The Edo Lear', New York Review of Books (24 April 1986) pp. 13-15).

And, discussing the distancing of Shakespeare's play by radically altering its setting, Kott says:

> ... in Shakespeare's dramas, the other place – the other 'historicity' outside Elizabethan England – gives, at the same time, the plays' other universality. And what is more, the place often supplies their other contemporary meanings ... The farther the 'other' setting in Shakespeare's dramas is from Elizabethan England, the less likely it is that the image will match the text. It stops being an illustration and becomes its essence and sign.

It's 'essence' and 'sign'! The whole assumption of these words is that it is possible to retain a play's essence by changing its 'sign'. Indeed, it is by changing its sign that its essence is both retained and enlarged. It is through a classic's imaginative metamorphosis that its eternal verities shine through. And, I would say, the reverse proposition is also true: that through the attempt to contain those verities in their original enclosure they become attenuated and reduced. Because, as one generation supplants another, as new ideas force us to test the validity, or at least the durability, of the old ones, artists are obliged to verify or nullify what they find in the old works. This 'verification' or 'nullification' is what determines the nature of the new work – and, in an inexplicable way, it often reinforces the integrity of the original.

The advantage that films have over plays is that the medium insists that the original material be rethought and then expressed differently. The disadvantage in the theatre is that there is a kind of premium put on some abstract notion called 'fidelity' – which from the standpoint of the purists seems again to mean 'make the omelette but don't break the eggs'. The only fidelity that cuts any ice in the theatre is a director's fidelity to his personal perceptions about a classic; how well and how truly he can put on stage the visions the play has evoked in his imagination. How much of those visions have to do with him and how much with Shakespeare remains an inexhaustible moot point. The central point, it seems to me, and the one that determines the validity or nullity of the final result is: what added dimensions does the director bring to the original work? If, as is so often the case, a director's imagination falls short of the work he is trying to realise, then he deserves all the calumny which is gleefully heaped upon his head. If he manages to transcend it – and makes something of it that was never expected and never seen before – he has enriched a classic. And if the word 'classic' has any meaning at all it must refer to a work which is able to *mean again*, and perhaps mean something else.

To combat such subversive ideas we have the counter-argument succinctly put by Maynard Mack. He writes:

> The most obvious result of subtextualizing is that the director and (possibly) actor are encouraged to assume the same level of authority as the author. The sound notion that there is a life to which the words give life can with very little stretching be made to mean that the words the author set down are themselves simply a search for the true play, which the director must intuit in, through, and under them.

Once he has done so, the words become to a degree expend-
able ... In the hands of many directors in today's theatre,
where the director is a small god, subtext easily becomes a
substitute for text and a license for total directorial subjectivity. (Maynard Mack, *King Lear In Our Time* (Berkeley,
1965; London, 1966))

For Maynard Mack and others of his ilk, the play is a 'given' and
as such, there is a tacit obligation to deliver its original intentions. For contemporary directors, it is an invitation to undergo
process, and only when *that* is done can its 'meaning' be understood, and because theatrical process is inextricable from contemporary sensibility, the play is either proven or disproven
through the act of interpretation. When Antonin Artaud ex-
claimed: 'No more masterpieces', he not only meant we must
lose our myopic reverence for classics, he also meant that the
present, like a Court of Appeal, must confirm or deny the pre-
sumed greatness of a 'masterwork'. The hard evidence for such
an appeal is the director's view of the work as performed by his
company and received by his public. Often in such cases it is the
interpreter's vision which is rejected and the masterwork, in all
its traditional greatness, which is confirmed. But just as often, it
is the artist's metamorphosis of the masterwork that wins the
day and, when that happens, the director and his actors do, in
Maynard Mack's words, 'assume the same level of authority as
the author'. To view this as some kind of usurpation of proprie-
tary rights is to misunderstand the nature of dramatic art and its
tendency endlessly to reappear in different shapes and forms.

There are basically two assumptions made about Shakespearian
production. The first, what one might call the Fundamentalist
View, is that, if a director cleaves to what the author has written,
delves deeper into the complexities of the text and discovers
more nuance and more shades of meaning than his predecessors,
he has rendered a service to the author and re-established the
supremacy of the work. (Many of the Royal Shakespeare Company productions fall into this category.) The second, what one
might call the Reform Approach, assumes that an ingenious
director, by interpolating ideas of his own, often far removed
from the ideas traditionally associated with the play, can sometimes produce a *frisson* – or 'alienating effect' – which is so
enthralling in itself that people are prepared to forgive the
liberties he has taken to achieve it. Set against these two, now

fairly standard, practices is what I would call the Quantum Leap Approach to Shakespeare, by which an idea, inspired by the text, but not necessarily verifiable in relation to it, creates a work of art that intellectually relocates the original play and bears only the faintest resemblance to its progenitor. There have been a few examples of this kind of work, but each so unlike the others that no general definition can as yet be formulated.

Edward Bond's *Lear* is an entirely original work, and yet it still feeds off certain ideas of class and cruelty served up in Shakepeare's original play. Tom Stoppard's *Rosencrantz and Guildenstern are Dead*, despite its autonomy as a work of art, remains thematically related to *Hamlet* and still operates within the orbit of the original work, where, for instance, W. S. Gilbert's *Rosencrantz and Guildenstern*, being an out and out parody, does not. You could say of Brecht's *Edward II* or *Coriolanus* that they are intensifications of certain aspects of the works on which they are based, but they still derive most of their power from the reference point of the original; whereas, in a work like *The Resistible Rise of Arturo Ui*, although *Richard III* is knocking around somewhere in the background, the play's historical vigour owes more to the author's assembly of contemporary political history than it does to the Wars of the Roses.

But much closer to the kind of transmutations I am talking about are works such as *Kiss Me Kate*, which can be seen as a brilliant riff on *The Taming of the Shrew*, and *West Side Story*, which uses only very general elements from *Romeo and Juliet* (social unrest, family feuds and so on) to confront contemporary issues of juvenile delinquency, gang warfare and ethnic clashes. In a film such as *Forbidden Planet*, a science-fiction movie directed by Fred Wilcox in 1956, one has all the narrative threads and many of the relationships from *The Tempest* without the director actually treading on any of Shakespeare's turf. Knowledge of the ur-text here may enhance a filmgoer's appreciation, but it is just as keen for people who never heard of the original. But all these examples are a little off the mark, for as soon as you have an entirely new wodge of material, a completely different format – that is, a musical form as opposed to straight drama, a movie rather than a theatre piece – you are really in the world of allusion, and that practice, given the habits of the Greek and Roman dramatists, is as old as drama itself.

Take a play like *The Tempest*, for instance. If you consider it from a contemporary standpoint, it is hard not to be struck by what we today would call its psychological symbolism. Connotations of the ego and the id have been read into this play for quite some time. Now, what might the fable of that play be if we remorselessly rethink it along those lines?

In a kind of private sanatorium stuck away in a rustic setting such as Surrey or Hampshire, we encounter a man who suffers from a curious delusion – not unlike Pirandello's *Henry IV*. He imagines himself shipwrecked on a desert island of which he has become the absolute ruler. Prospero's 'condition' has been brought about by the trauma of having lost his power to his scheming brother Antonio. To avoid the social consequences of that loss and to help him psychologically to assimilate it, he creates a fantasy world, and he peoples it with characters that relate to his condition. There is a good and blameless daughter with whom he strongly identifies. She, like himself, is an innocent, the antithesis of the scheming, usurping and villainous brother who, unlike Miranda, knows all the ways of the world and how to turn them to his own advantage. There is a 'spirit' that will do his bidding, exercise the power which he has lost. There is a personification of his own basest nature, that part of him which he recognizes as being full of vindictiveness against his wrongoders and which is, at the same time, the deeply suppressed *alter ego* of his enlightened and intellectual self (which not only accounts for Caliban, but explains why he threatens Miranda, that thinly disguised symbol of Prospero's own virtue.) And in this fantasy world, peopled by psychic extensions of his own enemies and ideals, Prospero creates a situation in which he can take revenge against those who have wronged him; can, as all psychotics do in daydreams, 'right the wrongs of the real world' through imaginary actions in his fantasy realm.

However, amidst all this delusion, Prospero is forced to confront his own inadequacies; that, in his former position, conveniently projected into the guise of the Duke of Milan, he was very ill-suited to his job, being more concerned with books and intellectual pursuits than with the humdrum business of politics; that, in a sense, being usurped by his brother was not entirely attributable to Antonio's villainy but could, in some way, be traced back to his own lack of qualifications. (Which is perhaps why he lays such arduous chores on Ferdinand, who is trying to prove himself to the virtuous Miranda – that fantasy projection of Prospero himself.) And when his delirium has run its full course and he has liberated himself from the irresponsible freedoms he preferred to his shirked duties and confronted the frustrations and aggressions of his own base nature – that is, freed his Ariel and rehabilitated his Caliban – he is ready to return to the real world: the world in which he must abandon his fantasies and assume his responsibilities. This is why he asks for his 'hat' – that traditional symbol of social respectability – and his 'sword', the practical weapon of defence which, from that point on, will serve him instead of his magical staff. The end of *The Tempest*, like the end of any psychotic delirium, restores the patient to the known world with a greater measure of self-awareness than when he left it.

Now this remorselessly Freudian reading of Shakespeare's play, I would suggest, can be played out in a single, contemporary room, in modern dress, with Prospero on a couch and a silent psychiatrist alongside, without any magical or spectacular accoutrements, with a few bits of furniture and some salient bits of modern attire to dramatise our protagonist's voyage from fantasy to reality. As a reading of the play, this is as valid as setting the play on another planet with all the characters in spacesuits (as has been done in several American university productions), or setting it on a Caribbean island full of characters drawn from a turn-of-the-century naval battalion, with Caliban as an insubordinate military lout and Ariel as Prospero's dutiful cabin-boy. For in all these far-fetched extrapolations of Shakespeare's play, there is some unmistakable line, which, stretched as it may be to breaking-point, still connects up to the themes and ideas contained in the original material. The validity or nullity of these far-ranging interpretations depends on the consistency of a director's *mise-en-scène*: how much of a piece he can make of that vision which he sees staring back at him when he gazes into the ruffled pool of Shakespeare's play.

Let us take another example – *A Midsummer Night's Dream*, which itself has gone through quite a few permutations, and was recently transmogrified by Woody Allen in the film, *A Midsummer Night's Sex Comedy* – and if Woody Allen can reinterpret Shakespeare, one wonders with trepidation, can Mel Brooks be far behind? We had had dark *Dreams* that emphasised the labyrinth of the forest, and bright *Dreams*, like Peter Brook's magically Meyerholdian version of 1970 and, inevitably, throwbacks to rustic *Dreams*, where the nineteenth-century version of the play seemed to forcibly reassert itself. But let us imagine, drawing on the sexual mysteries contained in the work, that one chose to interpret it in a decidedly pre-Christian, even decadent, manner, insinuating rather than uncovering ideas. According to this reading, the story of the play might run something like this:

Oberon, a vindictive homosexual chieftain who exerts immense authority among his circle of followers in the forest, has tried repeatedly to wrest a beautiful Indian boy from his former lover, now rival, Titania – who is himself a homosexual given to dressing up in women's clothes. Titania's refusal to give up the youth or share him with others (which has been the established sexual convention) has incensed Oberon and caused irremediable friction between the two camps.

To wreak the revenge burning in his bosom, Oberon arranges through Puck (not an ethereal sprite at all, but a superannuated and embittered slave) to administer a potent aphrodisiac to Titania, which causes him to become sexually obsessed with the first creature he encounters. Because of his dotage and incompetence (as well as the imprecise nature of Oberon's instructions), Puck administers the drug to two of the four refugees who have wandered into the wood to escape the arbitrary measures being meted out by the State. This causes a series of promiscuous imbroglios, presumably uncharacteristic of the four persons involved.

Eventually, through guile, Oberon manages to appropriate the boy for himself, and Titania, now caught in the spell of the aphrodisiac, becomes enamoured of an amateur actor, one of several rehearsing a play in the forest, who has been transformed into a beast by the vindictive Puck. Having now acquired the coveted youth who is the unquestionable cause of all the play's strife, Oberon takes pity on Titania's condition, releases him from the spell, and the old, sharing homosexual relationship is restored. The wood, transformed into an erotic labyrinth (which seems inevitable, given the proclivities of Oberon and Titania) encourages the lovers to pursue their carnal and licentious desires until Puck lifts their spell. Once returned to Athens, freed from the diabolical influence of the wood and no longer forced into arbitrary bonding, the lovers settle back to enjoy the entertainment laid on for the Duke's wedding, but Puck, in a final act of vindictiveness, upsets the performance of the play, terrorises the wedding guests and reminds them that, despite their heterosexual celebrations, nefarious, anti-social spirits such as himself are the true rulers of the world, and characters such as Theseus and Hippolyta only its figureheads.

A preposterous imposition, I can hear some of my readers muttering to themselves; a travesty of a play that deals with visions of Arcadia and rustic innocence. And yet, as many scholars agree, the *Dream* is a play about forbidden fruits (no pun intended), about promiscuity, bestiality, the slaking of carnal appetites, all those irrepressible desires that society firmly represses in order to ensure an orderly perpetuation. Midsummer Night, as the Scandinavians know better than most, is a night of unmitigated revelry in which the most potent sexual and anti-social cravings are released. Shakespeare, being a bourgeois writing for a bourgeois public, had to cloak the expression of these pernicious desires within a framework of 'a dream' to make them acceptable, but it is a thin disguise and the whiff of amorality fairly wafts through the musk and the foliage. What is love-in-idleness if not an aphrodisiac? 'Idleness' means going nowhere, unproductive, unfruitful – sex for fun and not for procreation. Puck, a character derived from an ancient medieval devil, is the incarnation of our most demonic nature; an old embittered and cruel flunkey who delights in creating confusion and moral disarray. Like a superannuated Ariel, he is Oberon's recidivist, a 'lifer' who, unlike Prospero's sprite, can never have his sentence commuted. He talks about putting a girdle around the earth in forty minutes, but this is empty braggadocio; a pathetic throwback to the alacrity and fleetfootedness he once had but has long since lost.

And of course, the amorality of Oberon and Titania is reflected in the surface society in which smug, privileged, upper-middle-class youths play sexual musical chairs, and of which Theseus and Hippolyta are, respectively, the kingpin and queenpin. When they were themselves – before Puck's nefarious influence was imposed – they 'played at' romance and courtship, blithely circulating from one lover's bed to the other. Demetrius allegedly 'made love' to Helena before becoming besotted with Hermia, and Lysander effortlessly switches to Helena under the influence of a mesmerising aphrodisiac, but, as we know, persons under hypnosis can only perform acts basically consistent with their character. The lure of the wood and the spell of the drug merely release the lust and lechery which were always latent.

Even in the case of the Establishment figures, the scent of amorality is overpowering. Before the present distribution of sexual partners, we are told that Oberon is supposed to have lusted after Hippolyta, even as Titania did after Theseus.

The tumult in the world – vividly expressed in Titania's speech 'These are the forgeries of jealousy' etc. – which results from Oberon's feud with Titania, represents the conflict of the ordered universe confounded by the Spirit of Anarchy, and its concomitant is untrammelled sexuality. There is an even deeper reverberation: the opposition between heterosexual love and homosexual licence. Oberon, Titania and their followers represent the homosexual oligarchy which flourished before heterosexuality became the dominant sexual fashion. The phantoms of that older order still cling to the underside of life and, though active only under cover of darkness, they manage to exert their influence and project treacheries against the new social order. The carnality, the bestiality, the rustic romps through morally deregulated terrains, the vague sense of orgy and riot which issue from the now forbidden love of man for man constantly subverts the rosy-coloured image of heterosexual harmony which was the cover story, not only of Elizabethan theatre but of Elizabethan life as well. The *Dream*, like many dreams, is a repression of unacceptable sexual behaviour which, since it could never be stamped out, had to be heavily disguised and, as it were, propagandised out of existence – and Shakespeare's harmonic Christian monogamy was an obvious form of camouflage.

To many, this fanciful view of the sexual politics of *A Midsummer Night's Dream* will seem entirely absurd. And yet, every time I read the play, I kept coming back to this beautiful Indian boy and Oberon's fanatical desire to have him. I would propose to you that, fanciful as it may seem, such a scenario can be played out within the textual framework of Shakespeare's play, with virtually nothing to contradict it – as it was, in fact, at the Odense Theatre in Denmark in 1985. And that seems to me to be one of the acid tests of interpretation: if the play co-operates in its own seduction, both director and material are permitted to have their fling. If the play resists, puts up insuperable obstacles or simply refuses to play along, obviously the honourable course is to desist. Although, without meaning to give offence, I should add that, on certain occasions, I have known classics to be raped to their everlasting benefit. A few seasons ago The Karamazov Brothers, a travelling juggling-and-vaudeville company, worked over *The Comedy of Errors* to everyone's delectation; and some seasons back, in New York, a streetwise version of *Two Gentlemen of Verona*, full of ethnic vernacular and topical jokes, received some discourteous treatment which did not altogether go amiss. But whether convoluted within the original work or compounded into an entirely different work, the tendency, as I perceive it, is to scatter Shakepearian seeds into new soil and see what amazing new horticulture will sprout.

It is a notion that the diehards will resist with their last breath, but what seems clear to me is this: what is essential in the better works of William Shakespeare is a kind of imagery-cum-mythology which has separated itself from the written word and can be dealt with by artists in isolation from the plays that gave it birth. And, by insisting on the preservation of the Shakespearian language, as if the greatness of the plays were memorialised only there, the theatre is denying itself a whole slew of new experiences and new artefacts which can be spawned from the original sources, in exactly the same way that Shakespeare spawned his works from Holinshed, Boccaccio, Kyd, and Belleforest. The future of Shakespearian production lies in abandoning the written works of William Shakespeare and devising new works which are tangential to them, and the stronger and more obsessive the Shakespeare Establishment becomes, the more it will hold back the flow of new dramatic possibilities which transcend what we call, with a deplorable anal-retentiveness, the canon.

How to rape
2 Shakespeare

It has always struck me as curious that no sooner does one begin to talk about Shakespeare than one finds oneself talking politics. Despite the fact that Shakespeare is universally admired, in some quarters even revered, there is no question that Shakespeare is a political issue and, like all political issues, instigates a wide variety of opinions.

The Conservatives have perhaps the most vocal and solidly entrenched position in regard to Shakespeare. They want to 'preserve his integrity' – which usually means ensuring that the satisfactions they originally derived from the plays are faithfully duplicated each time they are performed. The Moderates or Middle-of-the-Roaders are prepared to accept a change of period or a shift in emphasis, so long as the basic structure and spirit remains in tact. The Radicals eagerly applaud the innovations – the startling reinterpretations which enable Shakespeare's work to deliver new sensations, whether significant or not, whether justifiable or not, the 'novelty of effect' being for them the great justification. And there is an even more extreme sect, even further left of centre, a kind of Lunatic Fringe I suppose you could call them, and for them there are no limits to the transformations that can be made to the Collected Works. Restructuring, juxtaposing, interlarding, collating one work with another; modern vernacular mixed with classical idiom; rock music copulating with Elizabethan madrigals; laser imagery and computer technology freely commingling Star Wars and the Wars of the Roses, turning the Histories, the Comedies and the Tragedies into technological flights of fancy. These people would go to any lengths to shatter our revered ideas of the works.

Each of these factions finds in Shakespeare a true justification of its own disposition. As with the Bible, the Shakespearian scripture can be quoted to prove whatever propositions are being

16

put at any given time and, as with politics, the values and temperaments of the different parties are usually irreconcilable. And yet it is the same thirty-six or seven plays that remain the living source of all these energetic divisions. It is almost as if Shakespeare had authored a kind of Universal Constitution and, for the last four centuries, everyone has been noisily amending it according to their own lights.

I have to confess that some of the most contemptible people I have ever known have loved Shakespeare, and I have found them very hard to take. It is like sharing your bed with bigots, junkies and bores. For many of them, Shakespeare was a confirmation of their world-view. The Christian Universe was memorialised in his work and, from his sentiments, they would easily justify their bourgeois smugness, their conventionality and their pompous morality. For them, it was as if Shakespeare wrote only so that they could quote his aphorisms on their calendars.

Some of the most imbecilic people I have ever met regularly burnt incense at the Bard's altar, construing his works into eccentric philosophies and incredible modes-of-conduct. They believed, for instance, that *Hamlet* was a grandiloquent justification for doing nothing, for being, as one person once put it to me, 'eloquently unemployed'. Or that *Lear* was really about the pitfalls of social security and the old-age pension – and that, unless we began to take better care of our senior citizens, we would always be plagued by natural disasters such as storms, hurricanes and earthquakes. One ditsy old lady who never went to bed without her First Folio at her side believed that Shakespeare was simply the reincarnation of St Mark – and had proved through copious research that the Collected Works were merely the Gospel of St Mark in dramatic form. When I was in the army, I had a commanding officer who believed that Shakespeare was the guiding spirit behind military technology and that, were he alive today, he would be an outspoken advocate of nuclear warfare. 'Why even his last words were belligerent and hawkish: "Blessed be the man that spares these stones. And cursed be he that moves my bones!"'

Well, you will say, there are cranks everywhere, in all fields. But what can one say about the weirdos integral to the Shakespeare Establishment itself; I mean the people who write learned discourses on 'The Erotic Influence of Semi-Colons in The First Folio', or publish theses on subjects such as: 'Did Prince Hamlet Cut Classes While Enrolled at Wittenberg University?' or 'Was

There Chewing Gum Stuck Under The Seats of The Globe Playhouse?' For all these people, Shakespeare is, as he is for me, a living presence and a constant stimulus. But it does make one stop and wonder whether Shakespeare is really a kind of irresistible magnet only for the mad and deluded people of the world and that only those who claim to be impervious to his spell are the normal ones.

Let me pass on to describe some of the work that I have conducted with the plays of William Shakespeare, both in London, on the Continent and in America. The first of these classical experiments took place in the mid-sixties when I was connected with Peter Brook and the Royal Shakespeare Experimental group. We had been exploring the possibility of conveying theatrical meaning without relying on narrative. This was a time when there was a general dissatisfaction with 'the word' and everyone from John Cage through William Burroughs to Merce Cunningham was extolling the virtues of chance, random factors, fragmentation and discontinuity. Would it be possible, we conjectured, to convey some of the nuances and insights which are to be found in *Hamlet* through a kind of cut-up of the work which thoroughly abandoned its sequential story-line, which transmitted the play in bits and pieces, the way glistening shards of glass catch the eye of a spectator in a mobile? And what would flashes from the play look like if seen from the vantage-point of the central character – that is to say, distorted and exaggerated as they might be in the mind of a highly pressured young man with neurotic tendencies, suffering from delusions and aberrations?

The result was an eighty-minute collage stitched together from random sections of the play and wedged into an arbitrary structure – namely the soliloquy, 'How all occasions do inform against me': the one that, perhaps more than any other, expresses the schizoid nature of the play's central character. More interesting than the reassembly of the work itself was the challenge it threw down to actors who usually worked according to the rules of Aristotelian unity, building their performances from beginning to middle to end. Here they were asked to swing drastically, from a moment on the battlements to the Closet Scene, to the Play Scene, to the Court Scene; juxtaposing moments of pathos with low comedy, shuttling between lyricism and rhetoric, intrigue and satire. Nothing would last, for instance, for more than two or three minutes; no scene would develop to a logical conclusion, because no sooner was it begun than it was intersected by another; no sooner did a character present himself than he was supplanted by another. The play, like a moving mosaic, continually contrasted rhythms, moods, characters and situations. And built into the exercise was not only the play itself, but the adaptor's attitude to the play. Critical comment and, as it were, footnotes also had to be dramatised, since the academic perception of the play over almost 400 years was also a factor in the performance.

When an early version was performed at the Akademie de Kunste it was soundly thrashed by the Berlin critic Friedrich Luft, who took it to be a travesty of the original work. Almost immediately, a large number of Berlin students rebutted Mr Luft's review and, in demonstrations outside the theatre, circulated broadsides against his notice. As is so often the case in the heat of controversies, it was defended for virtues it did not possess, and damned for faults which were the very features for which it had been assembled in the first place. Again, Shakespeare served to nourish a political dispute – the conservatives deploring the dismantling of the classical text and feeling their world-view was being threatened, the radicals championing it in the name of some kind of vaguely defined aesthetic reform. It became fashionable to say that, if you already knew *Hamlet*, this was a fascinating recension which would provide a kind of salutary shock. But the fact is the collage was played before thousands of people who had never read *Hamlet* or seen the film, and their impressions (derived from discussions after the performance) were as valid and often as knowledgeable as those of scholars and veteran theatre-goers – because, as I have always contended, there is a kind of cultural smear of Hamlet in our collective unconscious and we grow up knowing *Hamlet* even if we have never read it, never seen the film or attended any stage performance. The 'myth' of the play is older than the play itself, and the play's survival in the modern imagination draws on that myth. When one assembles a collage version of the play – or an anti-narrative gambol through its themes and issues – one reactivates the 'myth' in such a way that people are reminded of it again. The collage was not simply a gratuitous stylistic exercise, a way of demonstrating methods of dramatic discontinuity and fragmentation. I held a very particular view of Hamlet. I literally hated what Hamlet stood for and still do: his loquacious moralising, which was only a pretext for cowardice, for inaction; his intellectualisation of issues that cried out for the remedy of direct action; his posturing and his empty theatrics; his amateur delight in providing boring and banal acting tips to hardy old professionals such as the Player King; his empty bombast in the funeral scene where, incensed by the sight of Laertes's real passion at his sister's death, he feels obliged to manufacture a passion of his own to try to equal it; his turning Horatio into a captive audience in order to demonstrate his prowess on the sea voyage, where he contemptibly arranges the liquidation of two gormless schoolfellows – just as, previously, he had blindly and impetuously dispatched Polonius in his mother's chamber, believing it was the King but knowing full well it could not be, since he had just left him at prayer a moment before. In short, Hamlet for me personified the paralysed Liberal, the man who 'talks a good show' and has eloquent opinions on every subject under the sun, but who, when faced with a real challenge, merely wilts and wanes like the gutless piece of baloney he is. Without that attitude, that animus against the received perception of the 'vacillating Dane', there would have been no point or purpose to the adaptation. The jumble and anarchy reflected in the work's structure was probably part of one's deep-seated prejudice against the character. Being unable to take a knife and cut up the character himself, one did the next best thing, which was to take a pair of scissors and cut up the play in which he had been enshrined. And here, once again, while we are supposedly talking Shakespeare, we are really talking politics; for *Hamlet*, through the years, has become the sacred cow of the reaction aries. They adore his platitudes, they romanticise his sensitive nature, his reluctance to commit violence – despite the fact that that violence, *were* it performed, would be an honourable response to the greater violence committed against the dead king and the state to which his son owes a powerful allegiance.

In *A Macbeth*, slightly intoxicated with the collage format I had devised, I set out similarly to chop the play into salient pieces. Again, as with *Hamlet*, the action was visualised through the eyes of the central protagonist: this time, rather more appropriately, since one conceived Macbeth as the victim of a witchcraft plot masterminded by his wife, Lady Macbeth, the chief witch of a coven which included the Three Witches – a conspiracy which was made visually apparent by costuming the witches as Lady Macbeth's ladies-in-waiting and having them always appear together. Macbeth, like Icarus, flew too close to the sun, aspired too high and so was damned for it. Macbeth, like Faustus, sold his soul for advancement and, like the Doctor from Wittenberg, had to pay an infernal price. What more fitting punishment than a wife whose body is inhabited by the very demons which swarm throughout this diabolical play, and who, pretending to be a staunch champion and a loyal spouse, 'commends the ingredience of Macbeth's poisoned chalice to his own lips'?

In this treatment I was concerned, as many directors have been, with the peculiar knot of trinities that winds its way through the play: three witches; three murderers; three murders; hence, in this version, three personified aspects of Macbeth: the timorous, the imperious, the nefarious, and three separate actors to play them simultaneously – just as Lady Macbeth had her three infernal surrogates in the witches.

Viewed this way, the political, the moral, the Christian aspects of the play disappear, to be replaced by the metaphysical, the amoral, the pre-Christian elements, which, in my view, are more deeply embedded than the 'history' inspired by the Gunpowder Plot, which some critics contend was the inspiration behind the play. In a version which selects certain characteristics, others are necessarily ignored. There are many who contend that it is outrageous to approach *Macbeth* without taking into account the historical conditions which pertained at the time of its writing and which are clearly reflected in the material. But there never has been a production of any Shakesperian play which delivers all the goods. Interpretation means that you place emphasis on some things to the exclusion of others – that is why there can be hundreds of productions of the works without ever exhausting their infinite possibilities. It is carping to complain, for example, that Orson Welles's voodoo production in the 1930s was an eccentric or partial view of the play. It was no more eccentric or partial than Joan Littlewood's version which set it in the First World War, or a recent Los Angeles production which placed it in a post-nuclear world with all vestiges of western civilisation obliterated. Every production provides only a partial insight and no production, no matter how 'definitive', can realise all its potentialities.

The Taming of the Shrew, like *The Merchant of Venice*, is a play that always left a nasty taste in the mouth. Women despised it, because, no matter how much irony one got into that last speech of Katherine's to the assembled wives, it always smacked of male chauvinism. The play itself, shorn of the highjinks and slapstick which usually embroider it, is a detestable story about a woman who is brainwashed by a scheming adventurer as cruel as he is avaricious.

What are the principles of brainwashing? We know them well now, from the Korean War, from Vietnam, from certain East European societies. To brainwash someone successfully you have to deprive them of sleep, deprive them of food, dislocate their moral centre and refashion their values and, ultimately, their personality: to get them to believe that it is the sun, when obviously it is the moon, and vice versa; to accept the fact that they are worthless inferiors who ought to be grateful to their tormentors for their life and their sustenance. This is precisely what Petruchio does to Katherine from their wedding to the play's last scene where, in a situation redolent of the Moscow Trials, he displays the haughty and independent creature we encountered in the first scenes now transformed into a tame and docile domesticated lackey. The only way to present *The Taming of the Shrew* successfully is to shut one's eye to its contemptible subtext and treat the whole thing like a jolly charade. Of course, Katherine fancied Petruchio, and of course, the belligerent courtship is just a device which proves that opposites attract, and that indeed these 'star-cross't lovers' were really made for one another. And if, through such rationalisations, you can invent a lot of comedy business and outlandish minor characters, you might just get away with the show. But if one peels away all those arbitrary layers of comedy and looks at the fable naked and unadorned, one finds a play closer to *The Duchess of Malfi* than to *The Comedy of Errors* – a Gothic tragedy rather than an Elizabethan comedy.

I first adapted this play about fifteen years ago, selecting the key scenes between Petruchio, Kate and Baptista as grim, humourless demonstrations of man's cruelty to woman. To elaborate my points, I wrote a contemporary sub-plot of my own, in which a young couple, loosely based on Lucentio and Bianca, meet and enter into a relationship which gradually deteriorates into psychological and physical violence. At just that point where it reaches its lowest ebb, the young couple decide to marry, since the magic ritual of marriage is still believed to be able to heal the psychic scars men inflict upon women and vice versa, and no doubt, when their marriage begins to fall apart, they will have a baby to 'save the marriage', just as they married in the first place, to 'save the relationship'. The Shakesperian scenes were inter-larded with the modern scenes, and each story progressed separately – Petruchio's heartless tyrannisation of Katherine giving way to the young couple's quarrels, confusions and psychological mayhem. At the end, when a pale and beaten Katherine, now successfully brainwshed, is hauled forward to deliver her final recantation – 'Fie, fie, unknit that threatening unkind brow, and dart not scornful glances from those eyes, to wound thy lord, thy king, thy governor', etc – the young couple, now dressed in wedding attire, join Katherine and Petruchio in a wedding tableau which resolves both the period and the contem-porary sections of the play.

In that first version (there have been four since), the contem-porary scenes were oversimplified and repetitive of the Shake-speare scenes. We saw the young woman inflicting upon the young man – in a thinly-veiled, psychological form – the same kind of torture that Petruchio inflicted upon Katherine. In the second version, there was a certain parity between the young lovers; both were equally guilty of destroying the relationship and each other. In the third version, something in the human and social fabric was made responsible for the havoc between the boy and the girl. And in the fourth version, recently performed in Los Angeles, the cruelty and self-destructiveness had no apparent source – it was just something sucked out of the atmosphere that men and women generate in one another. It suggested that all relationships, by their very nature, were destined to corrode, because people invariably fell in love with figments of their imagination, figments which were then imposed upon luckless objects, male and female, who just happened by. It took me four versions, I think, to get it right and, finally, I have no desire to return to the issue. But the source of all these versions was the grim and dark fable that burrowed underneath that woefully uneven comedy called *The Taming of the Shrew*, and, despite the fact that original material was added, the themes and ideas were extrapolated from the words and ideas of William Shakespeare, no matter how remote they may seem to be in this description.

'Nonsense', many of my readers will argue, some quietly, some noisily. 'All you did was distort one of Shakespeare's perennial comedies and reduce it to the dimensions of a soap opera!' I would probably not dispute that, saying only that soap opera has become an inescapable factor in contemporary life – which perhaps explains its great success on television. Most people I know live soap opera lives. Further, I would say that to combine the mundane and the classical skilfully is to create a delicacy almost as pefect as a hamburger; and, to push the point even further, I would say that when a playwright like Shakespeare provides us with the meat, it is almost incumbent upon us to add the potatoes, the onions and the relish. Our job is to retrace, rediscover, reconsider and re-angle the classics – not simply regurgitate them. 'I re-think therefore I am', said Descartes – or at least he should have.

It is difficult, almost impossible, to come to a play like *The Merchant of Venice*, whose central character is an orthodox Jew, without bringing to it all one has learned and read about the Jews in the past 2000 years. It is difficult, almost impossible, to obliterate from the mind the last seventy-five years of Jewish history, which includes European pogroms, the Nazi 'death camps', the rise of Jewish Nationalism and the Arab–Israeli conflicts. Of course, Shakespeare had no knowledge of any of these things and it is undeniable that none of these factors enter directly into *The Merchant of Venice* – and yet, can they be excluded from the consciousness of a spectator who attends the play? They can, I suppose, if one is prepared to put the con- temporary sensibility to sleep and only fasten onto the fairy-tale elements of Shakespeare's play; if one is prepared to say of Shakespeare's Jew, as of Shakespeare's Moor, that he has no actual contemporary parallel; that a red-wigged joke Jew has no real affinities with an Israeli business-man or a modern Hebraic scholar – just as an Elizabethan 'moor' has no real connection to a ghetto black. But it is a difficult thesis to sustain, because there is a cultural tendon that links all Jews with their history (even their history in Shakespeare plays) and all blacks with *their* antecedents – even the 'noble Moor' who, though he knows nothing of Sharpeville or American race riots, is still subjected to Venetian racial prejudice and considered an 'outsider' in his society. Rather than indulge in those strenuous mental calisthenics which enable us to separate our contemporary consciousness from that of Shakespeare, I prefer to yoke them together, despite their ostensible incompatibility.

What had always irritated me about *The Merchant* was that contemptible trial scene in which Shylock is progressively humiliated, stripped of all property and dignity and sent packing from the courtroom, a forced convert, a disreputable father, a disenfranchised citizen, an unmasked villain. It was to try to remove those stains from his blackened reputation that I decided to re-order *The Merchant*.

So long as Antonio remained 'a good man', Shylock must be a villain, and so I set about putting Antonio's character into question. By setting the action in Palestine during the period of the British Mandate, one had a ready-made villain. The anti-semitism engendered during this period was mainly the result of the policies of Clement Attlee's Middle East policy, which severely restricted immigration to Jerusalem, thereby forcing hundreds of thousands of escaping Jews to return to Europe. The man who seemed to personify these policies (quite unfairly in fact) was Ernest Bevin, the Foreign Secretary of the time. By identifying Antonio with Bevin and the repugnant policies of the Attlee government, and by lining up Shylock with the Jewish nationalist cause, particularly the more extremist factions, such as the Irgun and the Stern Gang, one created a completely different moral balance between the opposing forces in the play. The Venetian capitalists and adventurers were transformed into British colonialists and the Jews into committed nationalists. (I materialised Shus, briefly mentioned by Shakespeare, as an outright terrorist and turned Tubal into a kind of Zionist front man.) Shylock himself retained a certain ambiguity, vigorously playing the caricature Jew in the midst of Antonio, Bassanio and their Jew-baiting British cohorts, but becoming a cold, calculating Talmudic stoic when among his own people; a 'man with means' who knows he can be most effective to his cause by not showing his true mettle, except when he holds the upper hand.

As a result of this restructuring of Shylock's character, and thanks to sections lifted piecemeal from Christopher Marlowe's *The Jew of Malta*, it became possible to arrive at that detestable trial scene and make it turn out very differently. After all the intolerable penalties are heaped upon Shylock's head, and when he appears to be closest to collapse, it was possible to reverse his fortunes by invading the court room with his own supporters, taking authority out of the hands of the British colonialists and placing it in the hands of Zionist guerilas. This done, the path was cleared to 'alienate' Shylock's eloquent defence of his people: 'Hath not a Jew eyes? Hath not a Jew hands, organs, dimensions, senses, affections, passions?' etc. The scheming British oppressors are annihilated by vengeful Jewish nationalists come to the moneylender's defence, not only because he is Jewish, but because he, like them, believes in a cause. For the first time in Shakespearian history, Shylock comes out of that trial scene victorious, and The Duke, Antonio, Bassanio and Portia soundly rebuked.

Of course this is distortion! Of course it is taking liberties! Of course it involves plundering Marlowe to revise Shakespeare to satisfy the whims of an intruding director! I have heard all these arguments for almost thirty years – and during that time I observe that Shakespeare has been renewed, rekindled and rejuvenated by writers and directors with just such an intrusive frame of mind: Stein, Strehler, Vilar, Besson, Brook, Stoppard, Bond, Wesker, Strauss, etc., etc. And what are all these revisionists intruding into, I ask myself – the Sacred Temple of Academic Purity which scholars, critics and teachers have attempted to construct around the canon to protect it from incursions of contemporary thought. Conservatism is the deadliest force in the world of art, for it preserves old sensations at the expense of new ones. If the Elizabethans had been conservative about Kyd, Holinshed, Seneca, Whetstone, Boccaccio and Belleforest, we would never have had Shakespeare. If the early traditionalists had had their way, every Shakespearian production would be a bloodless transplant of the page to the stage – minus the originality and ingenuity that contemporary minds bring to traditional concepts.

Another argument with which one is constantly hammered is this: if you wish these plays to say things they never intended, why don't you leave Shakespeare alone and write your own plays? Why kibitz your own ideas through the forms and words laid down by another writer? Of course, the assumption behind that question is that there is a clear-cut meaning to the works in question and that I, for whatever reasons, am ignoring or distorting it, and, as I have already stated, I think this is a false assumption. No play possesses exclusivity of meaning; the greater the play, the more meanings it is able to engender.

But the other and more pertinent answer to that question is that the theatre works best on the basis of surprise. On the crudest level, one sees this in thrillers and murder-mysteries, but suspense and revelation are as much a part of the work of Harold Pinter and Sam Shepard as they are of Agatha Christie. And with certain works of Shakespeare one has a ready-made anticipation on the part of the public. They have certain fixed expectations as to what they are going to see when certain plays of Shakespeare are announced. They get what they expect and they expect what they have been led to expect and it is only when they *do not* get what they have been led to expect that they are on the threshold of having an experience. It is that cultural expectation that swirls in our brains before the curtain rises on works such as *Hamlet*, *Macbeth*, *King Lear* or *The Merchant of Venice* which makes it possible for theatre-goers to 'have an experience' – to have it precisely because it is not the one they have been anticipating. Many of the works of Shakespeare, because they are so well-established, so often performed, so widely studied, provide the given circumstances for this salutary shock, and in a way that no new play could possibly do. An audience is often like the implacable face of a stopped clock that will resist all efforts to be wound to the correct time, out of an obsessive desire to maintain the integrity of its broken mechanism. It should be no wonder that art must occasionally give it a good shake to get it ticking again.

Many of these arguments stem from perceptions derived from the plays themselves and, in this regard, I must say, the nineteenth-century essayist Charles Lamb and his wife Mary were in many ways a remarkable couple. They were able to read the plays of William Shakespeare and translate them into simple, unambiguous and definitive narratives. It is quite an amazing feat, when you stop to think of it: a definitive rendition of what a play is actually about. I know few critics who are able to achieve such succinctness. But, of course, it is also highly suspect, because the 'stories' of the plays need not at all be the tales the Lambs found in them. There are a myriad of other tales from Shakespeare that could be hatched from precisely the same sources.

Take *The Tempest*, for example. Prospero, ousted from a position of social responsibility by his close relations, falls into a delirium in which his deepest fears conjure up figures in a fantasy landscape. His breakdown is experienced as a storm; his enemies as intruders onto a private island; his followers as spirits of earth and air; and his daughter as a displaced person whom he must protect by means of tests, magic and manipulation. As he moves closer to mental equilibrium he gradually reconciles the forces warring in his nature. When he is completely recovered he sees them as the mental aberrations they were. His abdication of magic and his coming to terms with reality therapeutically coincide. He has weathered his 'tempest' or brainstorm and is now no longer dependent on magic or spells – that is, psychoses and pathological behaviour – and is consequently, once more ready to take his place in society. A psychoanalytical tale from Shakespeare.

Here is another. In *Romeo and Juliet*, two impressionable teenagers are so oblivious of the political situation in the country where they live that they do not realise that, by violating their sectarian allegiances, they are threatening their own well-being. Rather than accept the arbitrary dictates of their belligerent elders, they forge an illegal liaison and attempt to outwit those forces conspiring to keep them apart. One allegedly perishes, causing the suicide of the other. To the very end, neither Romeo nor Juliet comes to realise that it was not the stars that crossed their destiny, but human vindictiveness, in the form of partisan politics. Which, in my mind, is what gives *Romeo and Juliet* its tragic cast.

The aforementioned *Merchant of Venice*, because of its curious Judeo-Christian undertones, is a play that can either be reduced to a Venetian squabble between two merchants or expanded into a metaphysical fable with overwhelming religious significance. It could be a tale of a man who personifies the entire Jewish faith and who decides to castrate a Christian who is himself the symbolic personification of Jesus Christ. Cutting off a pound of flesh 'in what part of' Antonio's 'body pleaseth', Shylock can easily be construed as a castration threat – especially since 'displacement from below to above' has become such a psycho-analytical commonplace. And since, at the end of the play, Antonio insists that Shylock become a Christian, it is not too far-fetched to assume that, in vengefully exacting the full letter of his bond, Shylock is demanding that the defaulting Christian, through Symbolic circumcision, become a Jew. Shylock's vengeance against the merchant is imbued with that same tooth-for-a-tooth and eye-for-a-eye justice which whips through the pages of the Old Testament, of which he, Shylock, is a proud advocate. And Antonio, who is so inexplicably sad in the first scenes of this play, is very Jesus-like in all the sufferings that befall him: bearing both his friends' griefs and his own; gentle, generous, uncomplaining, a loyal friend, a good and virtuous soul.

Only once does he vent his spleen, and that is against Shylock, when the merchant reminds him how he 'rated him' 'spat upon his Jewish gaberdine', called him 'misbeliever, cut-throat dog'.

But is this indignation not merely a kind of echo of Jesus's fury against the money-changers whom, during the Passover service, he drove out of the temple, overthrowing their tables and tossing their money in all directions? And was not Shakespeare himself influenced by the Passion Plays he must have seen as a boy in Stratford, and did not those biblical antagonisms seep their way into the work of the older playwright when he decided to depict a conflict between Christian and Jewish ethics? I do not say that Antonio is necessarily Jesus or Shylock the God of the Jews, but the conflict between the two men is fuelled by differences that can be traced back to those alternative religions, and it would not take too much rearrangement to depict the conflict in those terms. A theological tale from Shakespeare?

One could go on to spin the tale of Hamlet the aging playboy with a weakness for amateur entertainments, who tosses away a kingdom simply in order to impress a public that no longer believes in his credibility. Or if one fancied a somewhat more far-fetched tale, there is the story of Fortinbras, the bitter son of a defeated Norwegian king who, wanting to take revenge against his enemies, decides to impersonate the Ghost of Hamlet's dead father and then proceeds to subvert the newly-formed government of Claudius and, through spiritualistic provocations against the highly impressionable student from Wittenberg, instigates the harassment of the Queen, subversion against the state and the consequent murders of Rosencrantz, Guildenstern and Polonius – not to mention the suicide of Ophelia – all as an elaborate plot that paves the way to Fortinbras's own succession – by default – to the Danish throne.

Although they might astonish Charles and Mary Lamb, these are only some of the 'tales from Shakespeare' that can be woven out of the incidents of the plays. There are as many tellers of these tales as there are readers, as there are spectators, as there are imaginations to respond to their given circumstances and the blocks of language that constitute their structure. And what makes these 'departures' possible in one production after another is the immense malleability in the works of William Shakespeare.

There are those that are enraged by such extrapolations and variations – not to say distortions – of what they take to be Shakespeare's original meaning; those that contend that a masterpiece already contains a richness of contemporary parallels which, because they exist in the depth of the text and the breadth of the spectator's imagination, need not be tangibly translated on the stage. Indeed they would contend that to make one particular parallel explicit is to rob the play of a host of other, more implicit meanings. This is a persuasive argument, until one considers the very nature of stage production. For, in the theatre, the actors and the director's job is to make a play concrete: to make specific choices about decor, costume, textual emphasis and thematic interpretation. In the theatre, one cannot put on the stage a kind of multifaceted resonating-chamber called a *classic* and allow all members of the public to draw their own conclusions from it. The artist proceeds from conclusions he has already drawn – from his reading of the text. The strictures of his profession insist that he choose certain ideas, images and information over *other* ideas, images and information. Since there is no way to render Shakespeare in a pristine state (that is, to let Shakespeare speak for himself), since interpretation necessarily involves diluting Shakespeare's work by putting him through the strainer of actors', directors' and designers' imaginations, the search for parallels is an unavoidable part of the theatre-work. Therefore the public is always receiving Shakespeare-plus or, as is more often the case, Shakespeare-minus, but what it is never receiving is Shakespeare pure.

The overriding aesthetic question today is: what permutations and what contemporary insights can be fashioned from the body of work bequeathed us over 400 years of Shakespearian history? The answer to that question may involve the smallest fraction of Shakespeare's original work – perhaps none of his language at all and only some of the ideas contained in his stories and his themes. Or it might involve radical reorganisation of his actual materials – scenes, speeches, characters which are unmistakably Shakespearian but which, taken into other hands, are now transformed and put to other uses. Or it may involve modifications, revisions and adjustments to works with which we are very familiar – perhaps in order to remove some of that familiarity, or to replace it with newly-minted ideas. Shakespeare's political spectrum is wide. It accommodates the conservatives, the moderates, the radicals, the anarchists; it is as multifarious as an Italian parliament, as divided as the German Bundestag. But what it must never become is the exclusive property of academics. I would make Shakespare available to everyone – except the traditional academics, those semiotic vampires whose vocation is to suck him dry, and index him out of existence. Fortunately, despite their own sense of exclusivity, Shakespeare does not belong to the Shakespeare Establishment, and, so long as they can be kept at bay, there is hope for the future.

Over the years, our Shakespearian understanding has developed from text to subtext to ur-text and has now reached the stage of pretext – that is, a point where the original texts are being used as paradigms for new texts. What we most want from Shakespeare today is not the routine repetition of his words and imagery, but the *Shakespearian Experience*, and, ironically, that can come only from dissolving the works into a new compound – that is, creating that sense of vicissitude, variety and intellectual vigour with which the author himself confronted his own time.

We need not be Shakespeare to duplicate the Shakespearian Experience, but we do have to find the artistic resources in ourselves to duplicate his impact; and to do this, we must cut the umbilical cord that ties us to his literary tradition. To create the Shakespearian Experience, we have to re-imagine his themes and reconstitute his fables. The real mystery is not really who he was or where he came from, but why we allow his influence to inhibit our conception of what we are capable of turning him into. His 'greatness' is nothing more than the sperm bank from which we must spawn present and future off-springs. Earlier I discussed the myths embedded in his works, but the greatest myth of all is that we cannot transcend him. Once we kill that myth, we will have launched our own renaissance, one that, theatrically speaking, is long overdue.

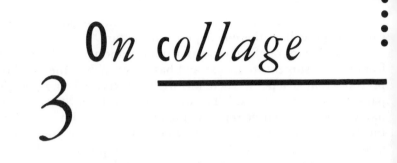

3 *On collage*

Theatrical collage (as in *The Marowitz Hamlet, A Macbeth, An Othello*) combines speed, discontinuity and dramatic juxtaposition. Speed enables it to deliver a maximum amount of information in a minimum amount of time. Discontinuity permits it to express interior meanings that in more conventional structures are revealed through the more plodding movements of unfolding psychology. Dramatic juxtapositions enable it to convey contrast and contradiction in such a way as to provide more dramatic information than is possible through sequential development. The effect of this swift, fragmentary method is to generate a surreal style that communicates experience from a subjective standpoint, thereby shifting the focus of events from an exterior to an interior reality.

Although in form and approach collage eschews psychological realism, within the confines of each of its brief segments, the laws of verifiable human conduct apply. Like a painter's collage, whose overall effect is odd and disorienting, each individual piece is made up of recognisable elements that, extracted from its context, appear as real objects in a known world. It is this fusion of disparate, realistic content in the midst of surreal form that poses the greatest problem for actors, as it enjoins them to express moments of true feeling while tied to the wheel of swiftly changing rhythms and to be as faithful to the truth of those moments as they are to the tempi that drive them from one to the other.

Discontinuity, if it is only an arbitrary division of Aristotelian time, is nothing more than a gratuitous stylistic device. A film, for example, that wilfully uses flashbacks and flash-forwards to convey what is essentially a progressive storyline is not really a departure from conventional narrative form. It is only when the accumulation of dramatic strands does *not* make up the sum total of their parts that we have successfully escaped the stranglehold of narrative. However, if that succeeds only in producing obscurity, it confers no boon. The dramatic value of discontinuity, particularly in the case of classics, is that it provides a useful by-product of the continuous narrative from which it has been derived. An effective way of retelling a story whose main strands are generally known is to skim its surface, re-angle its moving parts, and abstract it just enough to provide a new and unexpected vantage point on the original.

In Shakespeare, collage techniques are more or less restricted to known quantities, that is, plays that have become generally familiar through frequent repetition. In those cases, there is a certain dramatic plus in the act of re-ordering the material. Because of altered sequence, it becomes possible to posit certain insights or transmit certain ideas which, in the flow of the original narrative, tend to get lost in the shuffle of predictable continuity. The expected militates against the arrival of the unexpected. The effect of novelty is, at one and the same time, the greatest strength of collage and its most treacherous pitfall. In Shakespeare, if the re-ordering of sequence is at the service of a dramatic idea which could just as readily be expressed in the original form, then directors and adaptors are merely 'playing at' collage – not using it to renew or rethink the work in question.

In the case of the aforementioned 'known quantities', the collage technique, as I have said, is predicated on a knowledge of the original, although this does not have to be a detailed or comprehensive knowledge. It is enough for members of an audience to know the gist of the piece being restructured or to have a general knowledge of its given attributes. Although I have not explored this myself, it strikes me that it is just as feasible to 'collage' a more obscure work of Shakespeare or Marlowe, or even a play virtually unknown by the general public. In those cases, the insinuations of plot and character would have to be handled with more accountability. Fragments containing character features or relevant pieces of plot would have to be more cunningly introduced into the overall design, but, since the collage technique permits broad strokes of character delineation and fleet insertions of narrative strands, there is no reason to assume it is a technique limited to a dozen or so traditional masterworks.

When the material being reassembled in the new dispensation is derived entirely from fragments of the original work, it is important to point out that the feel and texture remains Shake-spearian and, as such, falls into the sphere of legitimate inter-pretation. It is when the adaptor appropriates alien or more tenuously related material that he or she must be most vigilant in retaining the unity of the design. Not that the appropriation of alien or tenuously related material is disallowed. Once the decision to reorder a classic has been made, everything is allowed – but, as T. S. Eliot said about *vers libre*, there is no such thing as free verse if a man is going to do a good job. The freer the adaptor ranges in appropriating new material, the greater his difficulty in integrating it into the work. Here the organ trans-plant theory fiercely applies. In order for the new or alien material not to be rejected by the organism, very strict selectivity is required.

We have thus far only scratched the surface of theatrical collage. Like so many innovations associated with the period of its inception, it is today considered merely a 'sixties phenome-non' vaguely associated with the cut-ups of William Burroughs and the 'randomness' experiments of John Cage. But, just as Dada resurfaced as surrealism and later as Happenings and Performance Art, collage, as a viable dramatic form may well revive in thirty or forty years and be jubilantly 'rediscovered'.

Since the most salient characteristics of late twentieth-century experience are speed, fragmentation and the mixture of antitheti-cal styles, it seems to me inevitable that theatrical collage will, in a matter of decades, oust Aristotelian structure once and for all. In fifty years, no playwright will contemplate 'developing' a theme through sequential narrative. Rather, he will coalesce con-trasting pieces that *imply* narrative development and concern himself mainly with the optimum dramatic effect to be had from the juxtaposition of its many parts.

Although such 'parts' will still – ultimately – constitute a 'sum total', it will occur to no one to 'add them up' in order to arrive at that total. The much touted 'bottom line' will be eradicated from theatrical process, and each dramatic numeral will have ac-quired its own particular significance. As a result of this linear (antinuclear) structure, the final act of theatrical performance will be the audience's and not the artist's. How the public orders the performance in its mind and through its feelings – artists' prerogatives notwithstanding – will determine what it is really about. In regard to Shakespeare, this opens up the opportunity for zillions of interpretations of the collected works – not only variegated subjective impressions on the part of each spectator, but countless new permutations of the plays themselves: con-figurations never dreamt of in Shakespeare's philosophy, or anyone else's.

Directed by William
4   Shakespeare

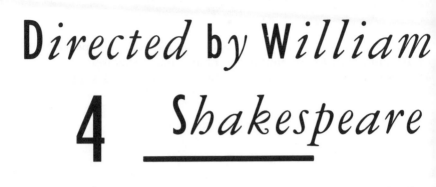

Thanks in part to Hollywood and in larger part to the general public's congenital indifference to artistic process, there is no commonly-shared understanding as to what a theatre director is or does. According to film legend, he is either a zealous bully standing in the stalls of an empty house venting his spleen on terrified actors, or a pulsating Svengali riveting his gaze on the young understudy and exhorting 'the youngster' to 'go out on that stage' and 'come back a star'. If the public looks for his work at all, it is in the more obvious elements of the physical production: the cut of the costumes, the feel of the set, the trick of the lights, the tempo of the performance – factors more attributable to designers and choreographers than to directors. Invariably critics will compliment the director for startling performances whose success can be traced back to an actor's stubborn refusal to bend to the cock-eyed demands of a man who knows next to nothing about a craft over which he has been given unlimited jurisdiction. Generally speaking, the director is some kind of nebulous presence which everyone tolerates on the wobbly assumption that every ship must have a captain and every orchestra a conductor.

Ann Pasternak Slater's book, *Shakespeare the Director*, tends to confirm my suspicions that, as far as the public is concerned, the director is the Invisible man of the theatrical process. Ms Slater's book presumes to divine the hand of Shakespeare, the director, in the stage directions of the Folio and Quarto texts, and contains chapter headings such as: Stage Positions, Taking By The Hand, Kneeling, Kissing, Embracing, Weeping: a veritable Kama Sutra of Shakespearian stagecraft. The book doggedly capers through the Collected Works, probing the meaning of this kiss and that kneel, this tear and that embrace, the pertinence of this prop or that costume-change – all the while inferring that a director is someone who gives physical directives, determines the cut of a character's attire and recommends which property he or she should bring onto the stage. These may well fall into the category of stage directions, but they are only the traffic signals of the director's art.

What a director does in the contemporary theatre, and what Shakespeare must have done to some degree if he ever did produce his own works, is to insinuate a personal conception of the material before him. It is hoped that this conception touches, if it does not entirely condition, the actors and everyone else concerned with the production, but the motive and purpose of 'kisses', 'kneels', 'embraces', 'tears', or the lack of them, are usually the arbitrary judgments of the man or woman attempting to co-ordinate all those variables. And printed stage directions notwithstanding, one has to hastily point out that there is a multitude of nuance, in a kiss, an embrace or an outbreak of tears, and that it is the director who determines the character of those actions by opting for one nuance rather than another.'

If Shakespeare ever did direct *Hamlet* (doubling as Polonius and the Ghost in the best actor–manager tradition of stealing the smaller plum roles for himself), what concerned him was the way in which the temperaments of his cast of characters could best convey what he understood that play to be about. As a director (and according to a certain school of scholarship, the Elizabethan director was closer to a prompter or stage-manager) Shakespeare would give every one of his suggestions or 'directions' to help realise his view of the material, despite the fact that the practice of 'directional conception' was not really formulated until the end of the nineteenth century. No doubt he would plot the moves, choose areas where scenes were to take place and propose ways for the material to be played, but all these suggestions, if they had any point at all, would be to further and realize his image of what he had written and what the audience was to experience. At base, all directors are arranging, not so much actors but the ideological blocks of the conception they bring to their material.

Ms Slater in her work cannily examines the physical implications of Shakespeare's verse, but takes exception to Harbage's view, expressed in his book *Elizabethan Acting*, that the Elizabethan theatre was inclined towards formality, extravagance and ritual. She deduces from the nuance in the writing and the inherent stage directions in the texts that Shakespeare's was, generally speaking, a realistic theatre. But I wonder if Ms Slater has ever seen a play performed outdoors – and, though the Globe was not entirely an outdoor theatre, neither was it a soundproof studio with flawless acoustics. When the radius of an audience is widely fanned out, as it was in the Elizabethan theatre, one of the actor's greatest problems is focusing a performance. There being no fixed centre to the house, there is, in a sense, no centre point for the actor. You find these problems arising with arena staging or in theatres with a wide, three-sided acting area. The actor is inclined to divide his performance equally between all parts of the house, being conscious of the fact that, if he lingers too long at one precinct, he is witholding effects from another. If this compulsion to share the action exists in contemporary theatres which are entirely roofed, imagine what it must have been like on an open stage, where the audience was constantly moving about, where vendors were plying their wares and where all the sounds of the outdoors competed with the sounds actors were making inside that wooden 'O'. In a theatre of that formation, all the dynamics of performance must be concerned with trying to achieve and hold attention against all other distractions. This is what conditioned the playing style in Shakespeare's time and, in my view, forced it to be larger than life – which, I should add hastily, does not mean slower than life. Speed of delivery is not irreconcilable with breadth of performance, and I believe Shakespeare's stage contained what we rarely see on our modern stages: bold, outsized playing at a rattlingly quick pace. The great audience predilection then was for flamboyant physicality. The duels were the equivalent of the big production numbers in our Broadway musicals. The alarums, excursions and crossings of the stage, the forerunners to the extravagant scenic effects of the nineteenth and twentieth centuries. The Elizabethans, more than most people can today imagine, lived in their skins. Their transport, on horses and coaches, involved considerable physical exertion. Their trades and methods of self-defence demanded quick instincts and constant alertness. And the stage, reflecting its society, was likewise tactile, kinetic, mobile and bounding with physical energy. The laid-back, room-sized behaviourist acting style we call 'realism', in such an age, was unthinkable. Its art, like its society, encouraged action, thrust, robustness, heady vocalisation and broad gestures: qualities which I, for one, discern in the work of William Shakespeare and which are in no way at odds with the subtleties of its thought or the elaborateness of its poetry.

There is in Ms Slater's book, and it is to be found in the writing of many scholars, an assumption that Shakespeare's meaning, when unearthed, lies like little krugerrands buried in the ground; that the 'meaning' of the plays are the scholars' discoveries of an author's carefully planted, *a priori*, intentions – whereas, in my view, that 'meaning' is more like specks of gold-dust compounded with coal and clay and other kinds of historical grime and, once found, can be fashioned into a variety of forms: urns, spoons, tureens, medallions or flying ducks. What Ms Slater does not seem to credit is that the quality which earns many of Shakespeare's works the title 'classics' is precisely that malleability which enables the same material to mean radically different things from one generation to the next, and that, because we are so far removed from the Elizabethan sensibility, it is sheer arrogance to assume that we can, using twentieth-century interpretative tools, deduce an author's original state of mind.

It is comforting to say that Shakespeare's theatre was, on the whole, 'realistic', but at the same time it is a meaningless label. The nineteenth-century melodramas, with their fustian and furbelow, were also 'realistic', in that audiences easily identified with those outsized characters and overblown situations. The heightening of style which characterised melodramatic acting did not nullify the realism of those plays; it merely inflated it. By the same token, Shakespeare's plays, despite the artificiality of blank verse and a relatively bare stage where the scene had to be imagined rather than constructed, were grounded in psychological truths which spoke to human beings in the seventeenth century as clearly as they do in our own. In that sense, realism, that is to say 'recognisable human behaviour', is the one thing one can never escape in dramatic art. Whatever its permutations, it is the only thing we know.

Still, everything is a matter of degree, and it is fascinating to speculate as to what kind of director Shakespeare might have been; and, indeed, there are enough clues in his work to give us a pretty fair impression. In *Hamlet*, we hear the voice of Shakespeare the director loud and clear, and it strikes me that it is the egocentric bleat of almost every writer–director one has ever known:

> Speak the speech I pray you as *I* pronounced it to you, trippingly on the tongue.

Obviously here is a director who commits the cardinal sin of giving readings to actors and who, like most writers, is obsessively concerned with *his* words rather than personalised expressions of his text in which the genius of the true actor is often revealed.

> Nor do not saw the air too much with your hand thus . . . for in the very torrent, tempest and, as I may say, whirlwind of your passion, you must acquire and beget a temperance that may give it smoothness.

In other words, do nothing to subvert or diminish the beauty and splendour of *my* words. Shakespeare – the director – is 'offended to the soul, by the robustious, periwig-pated fellow who tears a passion to tatters', that is, by the emotionally charged actor whose histrionic qualities challenge or overwhelm the supremacy of his precious text. 'These fellows are capable of nothing but inexplicable dumb-show' – or, to put it another way: kinetic expression of mood and feeling which rely on the actor's skilful use of his physical instrument and inner technique, which are often more eloquent than words – even those of our hectoring writer–director.

However, our language-obsessed director *does* permit gestures when the actor 'suits the action to the word, the word to the action' – that is, when he provides the crudest kind of mickey-mousing by which gesture reiterates the textual imagery. But he warns his mummers:

> . . . o'erstep not the modesty of nature: for anything so overdone is from the purpose of playing, whose end, both at first and now, was and is, to hold, as t'were, the mirror up to nature . . .

Not only is he helplessly saddled with the written word but a remorseless naturalist to boot! One can just picture him trimming the sails of Burbage's finest, most exhilarating moments with admonitions such as: 'Now Dicky, that was quite nice but a bit over the top. Just imagine how Smithers, the bellows-mender from Wapping, might deliver that line'. Constantly letting the air out of the actors' divine afflatus and grounding his most inspired flights of fancy, boorishly demanding that he show 'Virtue her own feature, and scorn her image'; that is, forcing the actor into that predictable, naturalistic mould which tallies with his own verifiable conception of clichéd emotional states. In short, here is the *worst* sort of director, hamstringing his actors' personal choices, strait-jacketing them to the written word and demanding carbon copies of his own authorial preconceptions.

As for Shakespeare's audience predilections, they are squarely with the upper-class snobs whom he was constantly flattering in his maudlin dedications. Unscripted jokes 'though it make the unskilful laugh' (that is to say, the groundlings, the workers, the hearty proletarian masses on whom the popularity of his theatre depends) would make 'the judicious grieve' – that is, the toffs, burghers, aristocrats and generals for whom he has dished up 'his caviar'. No free-wheeling interpretations loosed by his actors' untrammelled imagination and soaring into realms of extravagance and surrealism, only temperate simulations without 'strutting or bellowing' so as to avoid the charge of 'imitating humanity ... abominably'. *Imitation* rather than imaginative creation is the constant criterion. Hold that damned looking-glass up to Nature and do not wobble it for an instant!

And should an inspired Will Kempe invent some brilliant bits of business which bring the house down, our fastidious writer–director warns:

> And let those who play your clowns speak no more than is set down for them.

God forbid there should be a moment of spontaneous improvisation which reveals the brilliance of a comic imagination to the detriment of the text. But if an actor *does* raise a laugh when 'some necessary question of the play is then to be considered', surely the playwright is at fault for providing the potentiality for comedy in a moment intended to be utterly serious? Significantly, our author chides such a clown for revealing 'a pitiful ambition' – an admonishment which sits poorly on an author who can produce the leaden horseplay of Stephano and Trinculo in *The Tempest* or the execrable Porter's scene in *Macbeth*. 'Ambition', it would appear, is only commendable in the playwright, but 'pitiful' in the clown.

And what kind of theatrical sensitivity can Shakespeare have had when, in the guise of Hamlet, that impetuous, amateur Master-of-the-Rolls, he says to the First Player, the acknowledged leader of the acting company and a fully-fledged professional:

> You could for a need study a speech of some dozen or sixteen lines which I could set down and insert in't? could you not?

Can you imagine a writer–director suggesting that to Olivier or Gielgud an hour or two before a performance of a classic? Of course, the scholars will reply that this is poetic licence, a play-wright's necessary 'plant' for the sake of the coming Play Scene. Nevertheless it bespeaks a certain callousness towards the actor's integrity, revealed by a character in whom we glean those stage attitudes we attribute to Shakespeare himself.

I have the feeling that Shakespeare, like most writers foolish enough to attempt to produce their own works, was saved (and subsequently glorified) by the hard-working, ploddingly reliable Elizabethan pros who listened attentively to the gentleman's theories and suggestions and then proceeded to go their own way – a course taken by most professional actors when confronted by a fretting playwright presumptious enough to tell them how to do their jobs. Perhaps it is a great blessing that Shakespeare had no recourse to video or film, so that later generations need not recoil with horror at the theatrical gaucherie he would have inflicted upon the performance of his works. Mercifully the Shakespeare tradition in acting and production began three hundred years later, when the actor, and not the director or playwright, was the arbiter of theatrical fashion. God knows, if some Elizabethan BBC archive actually did record the canon in its own time, it might never have survived the next four hundred years!

:Stern

5 measures

One day in June of 1974, as I was passing through Selfridges, I came upon one of those cosmetics demonstrations which were occasionally held on the ground floor of that teeming department store. The girl in the centre of the group was extolling the virtues of a new cleansing cream that miraculously evaporated make-up. In a few days' time, I was about to start rehearsals for a small Grand Guignol effort called *Sherlock's Last Case*, the final stage direction of which read: 'The great detective's face, doused with acid, gradually disintegrates before our eyes.' I fancied that some concentrated form of this cleansing cream might provide a solution to this bedevilling stage effect. But it turned out that the product in question, efficient enough for its own uses, would in no way be helpful in dissolving Sherlock's splendid visage and so, after a few moments, I left the store, en route to the The Open Space Theatre, of which I was then Artistic Director.

A few yards up Oxford Street, still cogitating the problem of obliterating the features of the Great Sleuth, I suddenly felt two pairs of burly hands catch hold of my right and left shoulders and found myself indecorously hauled into a Black Maria which, as I later discovered, had been tracking me since I left the store. Feeling like a Kafkaesque hero on the brink of a nightmarish adventure, I eventually overcame the shock long enough to blurt out: 'What the hell is going on here?!' The policemen, who were making themselves rather over-familiar with my person, muttered between gropes: 'We're just taking you down to the station for a little while, that's all.'

At the station, I was told that I was being booked as a 'suspected person with intent to commit an arrestable offence' under the Vagrancy Act of 1824 – in spite of the fact that no incriminating evidence had been found on my person. I protested my innocence, became rude and angry, stood on my constitutional rights (momentarily forgetting they did not apply in the United Kingdom) and threatened to sue for false arrest.

If I were innocent, taunted the fuzz, what was I, a solitary male, doing in the midst of a group of women at a cosmetics display? I explained that I had a professional interest in the display, but thought better of launching into a description of the rather elaborate Sherlock Holmes plot as this might create suspicions of mental imbalance in addition to those of criminal intent already aroused. To make a long and harrowing story short, I had been spotted by a store detective behaving suspiciously (also dressed suspiciously, with beat-up blue jacket, red shirt, faded jeans, incriminating long hair) and so the police had been alerted and, after being tailed, I was duly pounced upon.

As soon as the police learned that I was the director of a theatre whose patrons included Sir Bernard Delfont and Lord Birkett, the tone of the interrogation changed discernibly, but the undertone remained: 'If you are such a respectable chap, why are you walking around like a tramp?' Eventually, after denying all insinuations of being either a pickpocket or a purse-snatcher and threatening them with everything from transfer to Ulster to excommunication, I was officially charged and released.

When I explained the particulars of the incident to my solicitor, I was told that, although innocent, I must be prepared to be found guilty. I could not reconcile this irrational advice with the sober and sensible voice relaying it. It was made clear to me that, because a store detective was bringing the charge, and her job was to spot and catch felons, there was a strong possibility the verdict would go against me. The fact that I was in fact innocent was, in some curious way, not relevant to the case.

During the next few weeks, feeling like a mixture of both Alfred Dreyfus and Emile Zola, I proceeded to gather evidence for my case: photos of myself making up actresses at The Open Space to prove my involvement with theatrical make-up; photocopies of the stage directions which described the effect I was trying to achieve at the end of *Sherlock's Last Case*; letters from performers attesting to both my interest and expertise in theatrical cosmetics, etc. I half toyed with the idea of affadavits from co-workers affirming my honesty and upright character but gradually realised the ludicrousness of such a course. Suddenly I was placed in the position of having to convince an anonymous magistrate that I was not the sort of person that would try to lift ladies' handbags and, frankly, I did not know where to start.

This, of course, gave way to self-doubts. *Had* I ever stolen anything? Yes, as an adolescent, I had once sequestered a second-hand copy of Robert Louis Stevenson's *Kidnapped* from a murky little bookstore in the lower east side of New York. Should I perhaps confess to that theft? Would it confirm my veracity in this case? Should I perhaps offer to compensate the bookshop? But that was twenty years ago and the book was probably worth all of a quarter. The insidious toing and froing inner monologue was worthy of Raskolnikov and it took all my considerable will-power to get it under control.

After awaiting trial for about six weeks, it was over in a matter of moments. I was acquitted and awarded costs. The police were gently rapped on the knuckles but, on the whole, treated with immense cordiality, the magistrate appearing to be highly solici-tous of their continued good opinion. Irrationally, I waited for the store detective (a girl in her early twenties who had testified against me) to come forward, admit her mistake, and apologise, but the look on her face simply said: 'Well, this one slipped through the net, now back to the hunt.'

Shortly after this escapade I was asked by a continental theatre to look at *Measure for Measure* as a possible future production. When I sat down to read it, I found all the ambivalent attitudes to the law provoked by my case reawakened. I had always vaguely understood that the connection between law and justice was strictly semantic; that in fact questions of right and wrong were not material to the conduct of the law, which was primarily concerned with legalities and illegalities. The law, if you were a criminal, was something to elude; if a solicitor, something to outwit; if an ordinary citizen, something to avoid. Like crime itself, it could be used to get its own way, and, being a weapon, the important thing was who held it and for what purpose it was being used.

The Selfridges incident made concrete ill-defined attitudes already roused by council run-ins, censorship hassles and the turbulent experience of living in a socially agitated Britain. It drove home the point that we are all in the gravitational tug of the law – even if our greatest preoccupation is only the parking fine or the fear of losing sovereignty in the EEC. The legal context is the furniture of the social context and we sprawl on it every day of our lives. In that very special, all-pervasive sense, there is no escaping the law.

Many of us tend to conceive of the law as an impartial tribunal which has been grandly created to adjudicate between right and wrong without fully taking into account that the adjudicator, being human, is as prone to biases and prejudices as any of the offenders hauled before him. 'I do not deny' says Angelo, 'The jury, passing on the prisoner's life, / May in the sworn twelve have a thief or two / Guiltier than him they try; what's open made to justice, / That justice seizes; what know the laws / That thieves do pass on thieves?' What is 'open made to justice': that is, obvious or alleged violations of the law, 'justice seizes'. What is less obvious – insider trading, undetectable sharp practices, 'sailing close to the wind' and so on – go scot-free. There is such a thing as a *patent* social offender who can be recognised by his class, his social attitude and his record, just as there is a *clandestine* social offender who, protected by privilege, has the resources and ingenuity to elude detection and whose crimes, being indiscernible, are not 'open made to justice'. And just as there are two kinds of criminal class, so there are two modes of justice: the vindictive and the obliging, but in both cases, the law is improvising, equivocating, compromising, rationalising, favouring one class over another, one precedent rather than another, subjecting itself to pressures from public opinion, social mores, the media, the government, the church and innumerable other factors.

The law's adjudications are the result, not of finely-discriminated questions of right and wrong, but of temperament, chance lobbying and human unpredictability. For one party or another, the law is always unjust and, given the grey zone in which it operates, it is constantly reversing itself, appealing and repealing previously-held findings and instigating researches into its own reform on the understandable premise that it can never declare with any real assurance how, at any given moment, it ought to be responding.

Deep in the bowels of *Measure for Measure* I found one of the few subversive ideas that ever trickled out of Shakespeare's bourgeois sensibility: that human frailty, fragile as it is, is still potent enough to destroy the fabric of man-made law, and, therefore, one should not respect an institution merely because it demands respect, but only in so much as it fulfils the ideals for which it stands. By *demanding* respect, the law uses a subtle intimidation against the citizenry, thereby protecting itself from criticism and attack. The 'trappings of the law' are not synonymous with the functions of justice and, to ensure that justice *does* prevail, it must be mercilessly scrutinised by the very people in whose name it is imposing its will. In short, a healthy disrespect for the law is the best way of combating its tendency towards corruption.

The Selfridges experience made me see things about *Measure* I would probably not have seen without it. It was one of those curious life-experiences which has a direct and calculable effect on one's work. It put me into a new relationship both with the play and with its author. It also triggered a train of thought which I will try here to recapture.

No one treated women with more exquisite cruelty than Shakespeare.

Lavinia in *Titus Andronicus* is raped, loses both her arms and has her tongue ripped out. Katherina in *The Shrew* is starved, abused, deprived of sleep and forced to kowtow to her tyrannical new master. In *Richard III*, Lady Anne, after a humiliating scene of courtship, winds up marrying the man who murdered her husband. Juliet, after being tortured by love, causes Romeo to take poison and is subsequently deceived into stabbing herself. Desdemona, for all her blameless fidelity, is suffocated by her aberrated husband. For loving the Prince of Denmark, Ophelia is publicly abused, driven insane and then drowned. The steadfast Cordelia loses both her inheritance and her husband and is eventually hanged. The list could be added to tenfold.

In Shakespeare's *Measure for Measure*, Isabella is wrenched from the cloister, threatened with sexual abuse by Angelo, and made to feel morally responsible for the imminent execution of her brother. After being talked into a humiliating sexual substitution with Angelo's former betrothed, she is put into the moral predicament of pleading to save the life of the man who tried to ravish her. This plea granted, she is coolly appropriated by the Duke, without regard to her own wishes.

In George Whetstone's *Promos and Cassandra*, on which Shakespeare based his play, the character actually yields to her sexual predator, then complains to the King, who orders her to marry Promos before he has him beheaded. After the forced marriage, Cassandra persuades herself that she loves him and pleads for his life; an outcome no more improbable than Isabella's sudden nuptials with the Duke in Shakespeare's version.

In my version, *Variations on Measure for Measure* (revised and premiered in California), Isabella also gives herself to Angelo (bed-tricks deleted) and the ensuing horrors that befall her are the results of corrupt authorities trying to protect themselves against censure and exposure. The wretched comedy scenes, with their noisome bawds, tinny whores and dinning 'What was done to Elbow's wife' etc., are expunged entirely, the Barnardine episode being salvaged as a piece of narrative stand-up comedy for the Provost. Claudio is *actually* beheaded and so Isabella's 'compromise' is cruelly futile. The Duke does not return to play a dual role as a stage-managing friar. When the heat is on and the city is in turmoil because of his enforcing dormant laws against fornication outside wedlock, he delegates his authority to Angelo and takes off. After Isabella's seduction, Claudio's beheading and the fierce restoration of law and order (that is, when the heat is off), he returns. He immediately realises that Angelo is guilty of the charge brought against him by Isabella and decides for the sake of maintaining the new draconian order that it is more politic to repudiate the girl's allegations and support his culpable deputy. He decides to make an example of this calumniating ex-nun by ostentatiously throwing her into prison and demonstrating that the new, reformed Duke will stand for no nonsense in Vienna.

In the final scene, having been stirred by Isabella's vulnerability, more so than by her suit, he coolly decides to appropriate her for himself. (Having been 'had' by Angelo, she is already, in his eyes, damaged goods.) As she flees from his embrace, her exit is barred by Angelo. As she tries to escape in the other direction, she is intercepted by a predatory Lucio. As she tries to avoid him, she runs smack into a reincarnated Claudio, in whose eyes she reads the same lustful intent that she found in the other men. As the regent, the deputy, the rake and the executed fornicator back her into a corner and simultaneously bear down on her, the lights mercifully fade.

Throughout, Isabella has been the helpless pawn of the law, and the excruciating irony is that it was to the law that she had turned first for clemency and then redress. In this new dispensation, Shakespeare's bid for Christian mercy is resolutely expunged, and the cynicism which takes its place attaches itself to the hypocrisy of the law and the duplicity of the judiciary.

Before objections are raised to this topsy-turvydom, it should be noted that, even in Shakespeare's *Measure for Measure*, moral judgements are consistently being blurred. Mariana forgives Angelo for abandoning her and sues to the Duke when his life is threatened – although Angelo, in no doubt about his guilt and the punishment it deserves, demands 'Immediate sentence, then and sequent death'. It is the Duke who is the perpetrator of this mealy-mouthed justice which will spare Angelo, so long as he agrees to return to the woman he has rejected and make her finally his wife. (An odd compromise: Angelo being landed with an obligatory wife – and one who is no richer now than she was when he threw her over for being without a dower – and Mariana with a husband who, besides being two-faced, is now proclaimed as a lecher, liar and cheat.)

In pardoning Angelo, Isabella says:

> His act did not o'ertake his bad intent,
> And must be buried but as an intent
> That perished by the way. Thoughts are no subjects,
> Intents but merely thoughts.

In other words, conspiracy to crime is not to be punished if the crime is not consummated, albeit attempted. Very few law courts would go along with Isabella's reasoning. But then, neither would they buy the Duke's notion of Old Testament justice:

> An Angelo for Claudio, death for death!
> Haste still pays haste, and leisure answers leisure,
> Like doth quit like, and Measure still for Measure.

Throughout, the notion of justice – that is to say, the social impulse towards righting wrongs – is compromised by mitigating circumstances: the bed-trick that saves Angelo from committing fornication with Isabella; the substitution of another prisoner's head for that of Claudio; Mariana's complicity in Isabella's plot, which rescues her from the opprobrium of sexually foisting herself upon the man who rejected her. Even Pompey, imprisoned for his pandering, will be 'redeemed from his gyves' if he is prepared to act as hangman for the State. Only Lucio is resolutely punished. He will be forced to marry any woman who claims he got her with child (and according to Mistress Over-done, 'Mistress Kate Keepdown was with child by him in the Duke's time' – and so *his* fate is firmly sealed). 'The nuptial

finished,' says The Duke, 'Let him be whipped and hanged.'
Poor Lucio, who strove to provide aid and comfort for Claudio;
who was Isabella's stalwart against Angelo and who defended
the Duke against insinuations that he was a hard-hearted
Spartan who lacked a sense of fun. ('He had some feeling for
the sport', says Lucio to the Duke in disguise. 'The Duke had
crotchets in him ... [He] yet would have dark deeds darkly
answered. He would never bring them to light.') It is the humanist,
the epicurean, the sensualist, the good-humoured prankster who
must be hardest done by.

Apart from blurring moral distinctions in his characters,
Shakespeare's attitude to the law is consistently ambiguous. He
who is entrusted with upholding the law, we are told:

> Should be as holy as severe;
> Pattern in himself to know,
> Grace to stand and virtue go;
> More or less to others paying
> Than by self-offences weighing ...

but this cannot apply to the character who is voicing these
sentiments, for he was responsible for promoting the laxity
which brought about the lawlessness in Vienna, creating a state
wherein '... our decrees, / Dead to infliction, to themselves are
dead', where 'liberty plucks justice by the nose; / The baby beats
the nurse, and quite athwart / Goes all decorum.' And, as he
admits to Friar Thomas, he was himself a libertine, loving 'the
life removed' and haunting assemblies 'Where youth and cost a
witless bravery keeps.'

Angelo, his hired gun, as it were, is supposed to restore the
order the Duke's laxity has subverted. He wants the strictures of
a disciplined society without being seen to impose them himself,
because, in so doing, he will lose the sympathy of the people. He
well understands the wily political ploy of effecting unpopular
changes through a front-man so that someone else takes the heat.
When the Duke was responsible for the law, lawlessness reigned.
When Angelo was put in charge, it was replaced with corruption. There never was a pristine state in which 'the sword of
Heaven' was 'as holy as severe – more nor less to others paying,
than by self-offences weighing'. The two poles in Vienna seem to
be licence leading to lawlnessness or undue severity leading to
corruption; the third possibility being the kind of Mikado-like,
punishment-fit-the-crime justice that the Duke restores when he

returns to the city. Under this dispensation, lechers are sentenced to community service with their old fiancees, the state is encouraged to fake evidence to suggest prisoners have been beheaded when they have not, brothels are shut down, playboys 'whipped and hanged' and victims of attempted sexual abuse appropriated by the state.

It was the irritating ambiguity of Shakespeare's concept of the law that I wanted to counter; to show that, in certain societies and at certain times in history, there often was unmitigated evil in the law and, when there was, its victims could not escape it through fanciful convolutions, but were ground down by its implacable power; that, in fact, a half-measure of malfeasance often brought down a full measure of punishment on those gullible enough to try to expose it.

The implication that, at base, the law is corrupt is strong in Shakespeare, but in *Measure for Measure*, as in its near-cousin *Merchant of Venice*, the playwright is obliged to resolve his action in accordance with the rules of The Hays Office of his day. Mercy must salvage wrongdoers, as it does Angelo (and as it might have done Shylock had he not been so unreformable), not because it corresponds with reality but because it is in keeping with the Christian dictates of a God-fearing Elizabethan society.

There is in Shakespeare, as there has long been in Hollywood films, a built-in tendency to resolve moral contradictions in such a way as to create a 'feel-good' ending. As if somewhere at the very centre of that rich, teeming, no-holds-barred imagination, there was a 'studio mentality' dictating what would sell in Pembrokeshire, just as it would at Wapping.

The strain of cruelty and perversity in the original *Measure for Measure*, though incidental, is unmistakable. It is not unlike the inherent cruelty in *Taming of the Shrew*, which also places an intolerable burden on its female protagonist and asks us to be amused by torture and sexual exploitation. In the case of *The Shrew*, which I also freely adapted, a particularly torturous personal relationship at the time caused me to see the darker aspects of what is commonly presented as farce.

Throughout much of my work in the theatre, I have found there is often a correspondence between my own psychological state and the material with which it happens to connect at any given time. In that sense, 'interpretation' has often meant transferring a personal paradigm into the classical work and using the objective work of art as the carrier for a thoroughly subjective preoccupation. What, I suppose, a painter who has to deal only with his feelings, his colours and textures, does quite unconsciously.

Free Shakespeare!

6 Jail scholars!

Free Shakespeare is the title of a little booklet by John Russell Brown, who has been Professor of English at the University of Sussex, and, during Peter Hall's reign, an Associate Director of the National Theatre with a special responsibility for scripts. His book has been widely read in theatrical circles, where it gained considerable respect – especially among directors who were actually tempted to put some of his ideas to the test. Briefly, Brown's argument is this:

A contemporary production of Shakespeare, circumscribed by a directorial interpretation, limits the scope of Shakespeare's work. In Brown's view, there is a wide multiplicity of meanings and possibilities in a Shakespearian play, but, when a director gets hold of it, he zeroes in on only one or two and, by so doing, gives us one man's view of the play, but not (what Brown believes was the case in Elizabethan times) a wide variety of complementary meanings, as wide and varied as the actors offering them. Although we may be dazzled by the brilliance of a director's individual conception, Brown argues that:

> When the devices are examined out of context and in comparison with the text or with those of other productions, they may lose their eloquence and magic, like a stone that gleamed at the bottom of a stream but turned dull and unremarkable in the hand that gathered it . . . Moreover, the difficulties of a text due to the passage of time or the complexity of Shakespeare's imagination, are kept out of view, so that the audience follows easily: they are conducted through the play as through an ancient monument, so that they pay most attention to those elements to which their guides believe that they can most easily respond.

According to Brown's approach, the director would in fact be largely unnecessary, because no ruling interpretation would be there to guide or 'produce' actors exploring the nuances of their roles through their own private imaginations. These same autonomous actors would then come up with their own theatrical discoveries and, Brown believes, this would produce a richer, more multifarious Elizabethan result. The text would adapt itself to the temperaments and imaginations of the actors, thereby freeing them from the tyranny of production, and allowing them to 'create anew at each performance'. 'The free performances of Shakespeare that I am advocating', writes Brown, 'would find a retreat to fixed forms almost impossible.' The production would be 'unfixed by detailed rehearsal and direction', but 'held together by the structure of its action'. In this way, Shakespeare would be freed from the stranglehold of directorial impositions and the audience rewarded with a fuller, freer, more legitimate, less pre-determined Shakespearian experience.

The basic premise of Brown's argument is that, if you remove a single interpretation, the director's, it automatically stimulates, actors into a series of alternative (Brown would claim richer) interpretations. But as anyone who works regularly in the professional theatre knows, an actor left to his own devices proceeds from his own self-indulgence to his own eccentricities guided by the manners and cliches of established actors and fashionable trends – not to mention the opinions of his wife, his neighbour, his mistress and his grandmother. Sometimes marvellous effects can be achieved, but almost always at the expense of other actors' performances and, invariably, at the expense of the play.

But, more to the point, the actor *wants* production, in so much as he wants a director to filter the undiluted stream of impressions thrown up in his own mind, so that he can discriminate between what is useful and what is use*less*. If the director has any value at all, it is that he is outside the orbit of the actor's imagination, presumably in possession of a little more objectivity and detachment. Far from imposing an immutable design upon the actor, the director monitors his performance, editing and eliminating as he goes along. He tries to find the most organic choice for a given actor within the framework of the collective production. The determining factor, one grants, *is* the director's overall view of the whole; but an actor usually subscribes to that view, and, in collaboration with him, tries to realise it. In most Shakespearian productions there is so much leeway in interpretation that almost any inventive or interesting idea an actor comes up with is hungrily assimilated by the director into the production. The director, far from using the actor as a pawn, actually depends on his creativity in order to get his own imagination working. The reason there is such a thing as a 'directorial conception' is that it encourages the actor to invent within a given framework, rather than, as Brown recommends, inventing independently and willy-nilly – as if the flight of the actor's unfettered imagination is always salutary, even if it propels him smack into a stone wall. Brown's argument suffers from an almost total misunderstanding of the director's function. The director is an evocator of ideas, not a blinkered architect working from an inflexible blueprint. The more talented the director, the more he manages to coax, wheedle, exhort and inspire results from his actors. He is the medium of the production – not its despot.

Describing his alternative method of work, Brown tells us that the actors would be given only their own roles – and not the full text of the play – and that most of the rehearsals would be in private study, so that the creative result would magically combust at the time of the performance, thereby drawing upon a wide variety of diverse experiences.

In the old-fashioned theatre of the nineteenth and early twentieth century, that was a very common practice. Actors were given only their 'sides', rather than the whole play, and told to memorise their sections independent of the whole. As time went on and actors became more organised and less slavish to managements, they demanded the full script at the start and felt the custom of memorising sides was an insult to their intelligence, and also that it encouraged a kind of assembly-line attitude to the production. Brown's theory begs the question: how effective could the spontaneously combustive approach be with Shakespeare when most actors already know the entire play in any case and have deep-rooted preconceptions about how it should be played? As for 'private study', this is already a standard part of any rehearsal process. To *remain* private – that is, away from the rest of the actors until the actual moment of performance – is to open the door to every kind of last-minute catastrophe. But the greater danger is that contact – the shared impulse between actor and actor which makes up the chemistry of the performance – would never have a chance to develop. Instead of it gradually knitting together through minute rehearsal moments, it would be expected to occur miraculously, when the actors first assembled for the performance. Again, Brown reveals a deplorable ignorance of what is perhaps the most vital factor in any production: the shared and edited experience of actors in rehearsal which methodically refines itself into the performance and which, as any actor could tell Brown, is different every single night, no matter how 'fixed' it may *appear* to be. That *difference* is caused by different audiences, different atmospheres, different psychological states on the part of each actor, different sets of preoccupations – personal, physiological and spiritual – which prevail at every performance. There is no such thing as a 'fixed' performance, because there can be no such thing as an utterly fixed human being. It is the thousand and one permutations in the actor's nature which produce the thousand and one alterations that make each performance quite distinct from any other.

Another one of the director's chief preoccupations is style: finding a style compatible with the production he envisages. It is possible, and today very fashionable, to mix styles – just as Shakespeare himself mixed conventions – shuttling between low comedy and high rhetoric, pastoral scenes and ceremonial scenes, violent action and subjective contemplation. In a good production, style is always a conscious factor constantly being sought. To remove the stylistic convention, as Brown suggests, is like removing the key signature from a piece of music. The actors, like so many stray notes freed from any given tonality, merely bump up against each other. An actor on his own, using his own intellect and his own imagination, can, as Brown suggests, belt out an original and interesting interpretation, but an assembly of actors all doing their own thing cannot possibly evolve a unified style. And, given the variety of styles inherent in Shakespeare's plays, the overriding requirement is to filter and define all those differences – not add to them.

Brown's conception of the actor's capabilities is wildly idealised: not only can each performer invent his own characterisation, he can also evolve a style which will marry with everyone else's. He does not need to be given moves because he will find his own way around the stage. He does not have to set the rhythms of interplay with his fellow-actors, it will all happen as a matter of course. Presumably, continuing Brown's own train of thought, he can also decide on his own costume and its period. He can play in whatever accent he thinks appropriate – so, conceivably, one can have an Irish Hamlet, a cockney Claudius, a Liverpudlian

Ophelia and a Swahili Polonius. Even with the most elementary examination, the absurdity of that kind of artistic freedom becomes immediately apparent.

It is significant that all the so-called collectives of the sixties and seventies which tried to eliminate the director wound up restoring him in one way or another. The Living Theatre in the US, despite its highly-touted communal nature, was created, guided and, in large measure, produced by Judith Malina and Julian Beck. In England, the Actors' Company, which was founded by actors, run by them and orientated to the actor's needs, found it necessary and desirable to enter into a conventional relationship with a director; the only difference being that the actors chose him instead of having one imposed by an outside management.

Elsewhere, Brown puts forward a case for what he describes as makeshift productions of Shakespeare. For instance, he cites a production of *Hamlet* by Tyrone Guthrie at Elsinore which, because of rain, could not be played in the castle courtyard and so, at the last minute, was hastily improvised and transferred into the ballroom. 'The production caught fire as never before', reports Brown, and his explanation is that 'Shakespeare's plays work best when a production is not fixed'. But the interpretative choices that made that production 'catch fire' were thoroughly fixed – not only at Elsinore, but when it was first produced with the same actors at the Old Vic in 1937. The improvised rearrangement of locale is something touring actors have to cope with almost every week, as they trudge from a medium-sized auditorium to a massive playhouse, from a church hall to a renovated tram-shed. The permutations of staging necessitated by these changes have nothing to do with the crucial character and action choices made months before in rehearsal. Again and again, Brown reveals a lack of knowledge of just how the professional theatre works.

But these are the more apparent strands of Brown's argument. What he is really saying, and hundreds of scholars have said it before him, is: Let Shakespeare speak for himself – without the intercessions of directors who cut, edit and rearrange the Bard's material to suit their own fancy. But the unanswerable reply to that is, Shakespeare cannot speak for himself because he is dead, and his writing only comes alive when it is resuscitated by the actor's imagination, in conjunction with the director's, for the mutual edification of a contemporary public. That is a long-

•

winded way of saying: the Elizabethan Age is over – not only historically, but psychically. The contemporary sensibility is as far removed from Shakespeare's as Shakespeare's was from the ancients', which is why I believe he took such great liberties with the ancients: because Shakespeare knew, without scholars having to tell him, that, in order to communicate to his own audience he had to adapt Boccaccio, Marlowe, Holinshed, Kyd, Seneca, Terence etc., because his audience had a different set of priorities and received the theatre at a different frequency. It is a trap to reiterate mindlessly that human nature remains fairly constant and that, because the Elizabethan Age was one of expansion and exploration and our own time is too, there is an inescapable similarity between the 1980s and the 1660s. There is quite literally a world of difference, just as there was between the sixties and the forties, between the fifties and the twenties; and, considering the frequency with which nations topple and thought transforms, next month may be the beginning of a completely new millennium and, this month, we would scarcely have a hint of it. The two overriding contemporary facts are speed and change. We have always had change, but now that we have rapid, head-spinning change, we must come to terms with the intensification of speed, the relentless, unstoppable motor power that makes the world move as quickly as it does. It is the rhythm of the twenty-first century which is already upon us which has to be found and reflected in Shakespeare's plays – unless of course, as a purely academic exercise, one wishes to try to recreate the rhythm of a different age.

The most repugnant of all scholars' obsessions is trying to recapture the Elizabethan sensibility. Even if it could be done, and I do not believe it can, it would be the most unrewarding act imaginable. Which have been the most exciting productions of Shakespeare in our time? The museum replicas in painfully reconstructed Globe Theatre conditions, or the custom-made works of directors such as Peter Brook, Peter Hall, Terry Hands and Trevor Nunn? Would one really exchange the swift, stream-lined works of the Royal Shakespeare Company for the plodding, romantic revivals of the twenties and thirties?

Brown's other major misconception has to do with the text. As I said before, the only way that Shakespeare can speak to us is through the voices of twentieth century actors and directors. They are the emissaries of Shakespeare's thought. It is all we have and, I believe, all we need. But language itself is no longer the plays' essential ingredient. It is their metaphysic, their sub-terranean imagery, that means most to us today. We are in-terested in Hamlet, not because of what he says, but because of the way the character connects with our own twentieth-century sense of impotence and confusion. It is his cosmic befuddlement that we respond to – not merely the literary felicities of his well-phrased melancholia. And the fascination of *Macbeth* today is that here is a character trapped in a diabolical universe of spells and witchcraft which connects up to our own obsessions with astrology and satanism, to the ubiquitous psychotic state that we encounter every day in modern urban sanatoria, in the exploits of people as dissimilar as Charles Manson, Jim Jones, Richard Nixon and L. Ron Hubbard. We are fascinated by Lear because we are fascinated by the agonies of losing power; of trying to preserve long-established values while new generations overturn them in our faces. That is why, in my view, a play such as *Romeo and Juliet*, despite frequent revivals, is intrinsically irrelevant to our own time unless we give it a very different emphasis. Very few people can accept the premise of ill-starr'd love and romance on which it is based, and that is why it only comes alive in modern productions when one emphasises the warring families and the milieu of violence into which the lovers are introduced. The plays, having been literally talked into the ground, are no longer language constructs. They are indelible images shaped and reshaped by succeeding generations and full of myriad associations, and when we go to the theatre we have an uncon-scious anticipation of those images. An effective production manages to illuminate that imagery in terms of our preoccupa-tions and fantasies. An ineffective production is one in which Brown's thesis is staunchly adhered to: that is, where we are presented with vast reams of Shakespearian language and ex-pected to respond to something called 'classical greatness'.

Paradoxically, Shakespeare is most 'free' when he is ensnared by a director and a group of actors into an imaginative frame-work which defines, with precision and much forethought, exactly what he might mean today. And these insights have to be found by scanning seventeenth-century material with twentieth-century radar.

The Brownian Fallacy is of course not limited to Professor Brown. Every so often, a band of mummers get together with an eye towards eliminating the meddling director and replacing him with a collective intelligence. The latest of these efforts in

England has been Kenneth Branagh's Renaissance Theatre. To fully understand the nature of this company, one needs first to understand something about the Branagh Phenomenon which, in 1988–9, swept through England and certain parts of America.

Branagh's most remarkable achievement has been that he managed to raise 7.5 million dollars for a film version of *Henry V*. This automatically gave him the kind of charisma that often attaches itself to entrepreneurs who, at a very young age, appear to have a charmed life. What made *Henry V* remarkable was that it had the strongest supporting cast of any Shakespearian work ever filmed. Branagh's interpretation, a young man whose coming-of-age and coming to kingship virtually coincide, created a dramatically viable alternative to Olivier's, and the entire effort, whether directed by Branagh or his chief cameraman Kenneth Macmillan, was entirely creditable.

The Renaissance Theatre Company is under the patronage of the Prince of Wales and the paternalistic supervision of Hugh Cruttwell, the ex-principal of the Royal Academy of Music and Dramatic Art. Mr Branagh is clearly a child of the establishment who has hitched his wagon to highly visible establishment stars such as Dame Judi Dench and Derek Jacobi and evolved a dogma attractive to actors who have had bad run-ins with conventional organisations, particularly the large subsidised companies. The Branagh dogma, like the Brownian Fallacy is: directors are not to be trusted and it is much better to let actors fend for themselves.

'I wanted to form a company', wrote Branagh in his autobiography, *Beginnings*, 'which tapped the imagination and energy of the actors involved, a company which placed the actors in a central position. If the actors wanted to direct or to write, then they would be encouraged to do this and it need not be at the expense of full-time writers and directors. It would be a practical realignment of the collaborative process between writer, actor and director that would step up the contribution of the performer.'

In England, actors have always written and some of the country's leading playwrights, Whiting, Wesker, Pinter, Orton, Ayckbourn, among others, rose from the ranks of the acting profession – just as many directors, tend to do. But, almost invariably, they proceeded to concentrate on one sphere or the other, very rarely, and not usually with inspiring results, have they plied all three trades simultaneously. It is not clear to me how the encouragement of actors to become writers 'realigns' the collaborative process between writer, actor and director. There has been constant interchange between all these functions for many years. What Branagh really means, I suspect, is that actors should be encouraged to 'write' and 'direct', whether they reveal aptitudes for these disciplines or not, on the shaky assumption that talent in one area can magically be transferred to another. But of course, this is the seedbed of dilettantism and, in Branagh's own case, the theory has been clearly disproved. (His own play, *Public Enemy*, got a rather rocky reception in London theatres and, as a stage-director, he has still to prove himself. As an actor, he possesses unquestionable talent.)

In preparing his production of *Romeo and Juliet* for the Renaissance Company, Branagh confesses in his autobiography *Beginnings*, that he 'made secret visits to the Shakespeare Centre in Stratford and read every prompt copy for each Stratford production since 1947, making copious notes and nicking everything that worked' – so it was perhaps not so much a matter of the actor unleashing his own directorial creativity as it was of 'nicking' extant ideas from the work of other directors. Is this really the kind of 'creativity' the actor is advocating?

Branagh seems to believe that, in order for an actor–director to function effectively, all he needs are some intelligent pilots to steer him away from hazardous cliffs or treacherous marshland. Having an inordinately short rehearsal period for a Renaissance production, Branagh organised what he calls 'some insurance policies'. 'I had already made contact with Hugh Cruttwell who had agreed to join the production as an artistic consultant, and he would be there to monitor my performance and to offer regular comments about the production. Russell Jackson, from the Shakespeare Institute on Stratford, agreed to act as text advisor.' I do not know Mr Jackson, but the spectacle of Mr Cruttwell, a genial, cautious and conservative academy administrator with no outstanding credits as a professional director, functioning as one strikes terror to my heart.

It does not occur to Mr Branagh that this eclectic approach to production can never be the equivalent of a unified directorial vision – but then such a vision (or 'conception', the more malodorous word) is precisely what he wishes to avoid. 'I wanted to see', he wrote of his company, 'whether fine performances from excellent acting imaginations could actually provide as much illumination for a play as a single dominating design or production concept.'

Mr Branagh, one must remember, was formed by the precepts of the Royal Academy of Dramatic Art and the Green Room mentality that encapsulates professional actors during and immediately after drama school education in England. The swift progression of rep, touring, occasional jobs in the West End and short stints with either The National or the RSC solidifies the actor's camaraderie and his belief in the pragmatism of the actor's art. In the midst of performing these jobs he frequently encounters 'conceptualising directors' who try to bend him to their own will, demean his integrity as an artist and force him to relinquish his own ideas for the sake of some larger design which may or may not have artistic validity.

Such an actor is ripe for revolt. Wiggle before his eyes the carrot of an acting collective, a company predicated on the supremacy of the actor and the elimination of directorial sovereignty, and he feels himself invited into a select revolutionary circle. It is a secret society that feeds on negative directorial experiences. 'I approached Anthony Hopkins with the idea of his directing *Macbeth*,' writes Branagh, 'and he agreed immediately. He was passionately opposed to bad directors and felt it was about time that actors had a go, and he recalled a particularly unhappy production of this play at the National Theatre, where everything seemed to have gone wrong, even the costumes.' Tales of smouldering discontent with established directors in traditional organisations feed the actor's hubris. Discussing the company with Judi Dench, Branagh writes: 'We'd had chats about the instinctive feeling actors had that they could do just as well as the director, and we had also agreed that fear would always defeat such feelings . . . For hundreds of years, for good or ill, the actor has been acknowledged as the chief vessel through which the play is understood. In recent times the emphasis has moved dangerously far from this principle. The kind of theatre which had emerged in the late forties and early fifties, and which had been pre-eminent ever since, had produced excellent results, but, in my brief experience, one of its chief failings was a frequent underestimation of the role of the actor.' This is, of course, the period that produced Olivier, Gielgud, Richardson, Scofield, Guinness, Burton, Quayle, Neville, Badel, Ashcroft and Tutin – not what most people would call 'underestimated actors'.

Essentially Branagh and actors with similar experiences are reacting against the dull thud of mindless British directors – a highly prolific breed in England. But it only takes one fertilising experience under a truly inspiring director for an actor to realise that his own ideas can be miraculously transformed by the voltage released by a distinctly different creative mind and, in the midst of such a collaboration, he learns how a seed planted in fertile soil and properly tended during a rehearsal period can produce vegetation that cannot grow by any other means.

Simplistic notions of actors reappropriating territory that is rightfully theirs and thereby avoiding directorial exploitation invariably go hand in hand with simplistic ideas about populist art or – in Branagh's term – 'life-enhancing populism'. 'We wanted to present popular art', says Branagh. 'Not poor art or thin art or even "arty" art but popular art that would expand the mind and the senses and really entertain ... I wanted to work on Shakespeare, but I wanted it to be accessible.'

Accessibility and populism almost invariably usher in facile, oversimplified results because there is a complexity in classics which resists reductive reasoning. Results come more easily because problems, rather than being confronted, are either underestimated or simply not perceived. Behind a first-rate classical production is not merely the desire to make the material 'more accessible' to the masses, but an attempt to convey a personalised view of what the material means to its interpreters. Without that charge of personal insight and the recognition that classical acting involves ingenious solutions to incredibly difficult problems, Shakepeare becomes that contradiction in terms: a lifeless revival.

The core of Branagh's theories was put to the test in Los Angeles where, in 1990, the Renaissance Company opened with two shows: *Midsummer Night's Dream* and *King Lear*. Although Branagh was listed as director, the guiding hand or conceptual-ising mind of a director was nowhere in evidence – which was quite consistent with the proclaimed dogma. The company itself came over as an ill assorted mixture of anonymous men and unattractive women, gambolling through *Midsummer Night's Dream* as if having stumbled on the masterpiece for the first time. Cavorting before an astral backdrop punctured with star-shaped holes (and on a circular acting area that encouraged actors to constantly upstage themselves) the company vied for audience approval by projecting high spirits and undisciplined physicality.

In a rough and tumble way, and relying largely on the play's textual comedy, the mechanicals' scenes worked most of the time, but the play's metaphysic was a pseudo-lyrical mishmash derived from every fairyland cliche in the book. The lovers were indistinguishable, uniformly brash and excitable, constantly demonstrating their text as if playing to audiences of the deaf-and-dumb. No distinction was drawn between the court of Theseus and Hippolyta and the underworld royalty of Oberon and Titania. The appearance of a comic notion of a Shake-spearian joke was heralded by raucous guffaws and mummers falling about.

The mechanicals were based on the stock members of a British amateur society, a choice which, though hackneyed, was inter-mittently amusing. The best thing about the evening was that it was crowned with a Cochran-styled musical revue finale which engendered the kind of upbeat feelings a company as impove-rished as this requires in order to obliterate its overriding lack of style. ('Love me, love my dog-of-a-show', they seemed to be singing.)

Richard Briers, in the role closest to his natural talents, was a nicely bumptious Bottom and extracted a lot of snide, in-group comedy from the rehearsal scenes and, in particular, his rivalry with Peter Quince – the role in which Branagh, playing the officious and self-important director, had his best moments.

Then Mr Briers, suffused with a hubris which is insupportable in what I take to be a low-brow farceur, proceeded to give us his pint-size interpretation of King Lear as a peppery old potentate directly descended from King Gama in *Princess Ida* who appeared to have spawned two daughters as cantankerous and spiteful as himself. Cordelia bore an alarming resemblance to Popeye's Olive Oyl and lacked all the poise and aristocratic strength which enables us to identify with this character's refusal to kowtow to her dictatorial father's commands. Lear's descent, in Briers' interpretation, was not from the hierarchical to the terrestial but from the ground floor to the basement. In a cruel perversion of the sympathy this character usually incites, we were delighted to see him soaked by the rainstorm, and prayed fondly that a double pneumonia would carry him off.

The evening's *coup-de-théâtre* (the anti-director deigning to include a 'directorial touch') was a circular spray of real rainfall which, as is always the case when reality intrudes upon illusion, tended to emphasise the gruelling artifice of everything around it.

Mr Branagh, whose smarmy rough-hewn, acerbic stage persona would have been perfect for Edmund, miscast himself as Edgar – and did nothing more with the role than project the traditional

•

tomfoolery of Poor Tom. One never for a moment believed in his filial attachment to Gloucester nor his manipulation at the hands of Edmund (a character ostensibly patterned on Captain Hook). Emma Thompson's Fool was costumed as a squat, hunchbacked toad – an ingenious choice – but was at no time in contact with Lear. It was a characterisation born and bred in an actress's far-fetched imagination and then arbitrarily tacked onto a few conundrums and philosophical ditties. Had there been a director, he could have told her at once that the Fool's separation from his master was a fault for which no amount of character ingenuity could possibly atone.

There being no intellectual framework, the storm was merely a meteorological event and Lear's trial of his daughters in the Hovel scene a madman's aberration with no philosophic overtones. Anything that popped into the mind of the actors was lovingly incorporated and, unfortunately, their collective consciousness seemed to be entirely stocked with the obvious and the banal. Neither Mr Branagh nor Mr Briers had anything to tell us about *King Lear*, other than that it was a great play easily mangled by actors' self-indulgence and trivialised by a repertory mentality that views it only as a series of comic or tragic vignettes. In a very real sense, this became a play about artistic inadequacy trying to come to grips with a masterpiece which eluded it at every turn. One was left with the impression that a group of actors with fair to middling talents had been encouraged to display their worst weaknesses and that, if monitored and shaped by a discerning outside intelligence, they could have produced something more worthwhile. Ironically, despite the abhorrence the company had for 'conceptions', it was the *jumble* of conceptions which produced such disagreeable results. In attempting to demonstrate one proposition, the work had merely reconfirmed another.

When, as director of The Open Space, I was asked in interviews what my long-range goal for the theatre was, I frequently responded: to create an ensemble intelligence by which the director could be eliminated. I still believe this is a desirable goal, but realise that, before a company can eliminate the physical presence of the director, it has to assimilate the conceptualising impulse and shaping intelligence which make good directors indispensible to the theatre. That is, that actors working in concert have to create an invisible entity among themselves which is the *equivalent* of the overmastering taste one usually gets from a director.

A company can get rid of a director – just as an orchestra can get rid of a conductor – but what is indispensible in both cases is a sense of rhythm, individual virtuosity, refined skills interacting with one another and imaginative interpretation at the service of a work of art. Whether the best way to engender these qualities is simply to let actors do their own thing seems to be highly dubious. In the work of some of the finest collectives of recent times (The Living Theatre, The Open Theatre, The Actors' Company, The Joint Stock Company, The Freehold) a judicious balance has been struck between writers, actors and directors. Although the director's function has in some cases been subordinated, it has never been entirely appropriated by the ensemble.

At the root of both Mr Branagh's work and Mr Brown's philosophy is an understandable mistrust of the conceptualising director: the man who, whether he acknowledges it or not, is using actors as pawns for the greater glory of his personal chess game. But, if it is a magnificent chess game and the moves are truly unpredictable, even the pawns are elevated and share in the match's overall success. If it is an undistinguished chess game, with standardised moves and predictable ploys, of course it must engender boredom or indifference. But (to pursue this metaphor to its end) can pawns, bishops, rooks and queens move of their own volition? Chess is the expressed strategy of a guiding intelligence, a perfect symbol of the dance of action and counter-action that you find underlying the best drama. Theatre, you may counter, is not chess. It is actors coming to terms with a wide variety of acting challenges – a process whereby individual initiative produces collective action which automatically serves the playwright's needs. If *one* conception is salutary, then *several* are even more salutary. Surely in this age of galloping demo-cratisation, the time has come to give actors the freedom that authoritarian directors have methodically filched from them over a period of about a hundred years.

The conceptualising director, if by that term is meant people like Stanislavsky, Jessner, Appia and Meyerhold, is only about a century old. Before actors, under the stewardship of a kind of stage-manager, assembled the pieces of a production them-selves. Occasionally, playwrights such as Molière, Guitry,

Brecht, Coward, Ayckbourn and Pinter stepped into direct their own plays, but, before the advent of the writer–superstar, it was the actors who made themselves responsible both for production and interpretation, although we have only recently begun to draw the distinction between the two.

The arrival of interpretative directors was decisively a step up – a form of artistic maturity which produced the eye-opening productions of artists like Vakhtanghov, Tairov, Reinhardt, Guthrie, Vilar, Strehler, Mnouchkine, Kazan, Grotowski, Brook, Sellars, etc. What the work of these directors confirmed was that a play, like a piece of music, could be made to mean different things when assembled from different viewpoints. The actors, far from being exploited by these artists, were the recipients of their instigating imaginations and, alongside every director I have mentioned, one can list many outstanding actors whose work was invigorated because of their *mise-en-scène*.

I do not say directors should hold a lifelong patent on the productions of pays. I *do* say that, during the time that patent has been in force, the theatre in many countries of the world has flourished. If one wishes to reassign the patent to unmonitored acting ensembles, there is no artistic legislation to prevent it. But until such time as ensembles can evolve the aesthetic wizardry needed to animate a work of art, the conceptualising director is the lesser of two evils.

A Response from John Russell Brown

Written in the early 1970s, *Free Shakespeare* is no longer in print and cannot speak for itself. I am sorry that the force of Charles Marowitz's argument has led him to falsify mine and glad of the opportunity to set the record straight from my point of view.

I have never supposed that Shakespeare 'can speak for himself' and took an early opportunity in *Free Shakespeare* to say so. I know that every age reinvents Shakespeare, and so I argued against 'museum productions', and questioned whether the Shakespeare of the late 1960s was modern enough. But the main rejoinder I would like to make is that I was not laying down principles for Shakespeare production, but proposing a very limited experiment, in a small space and using the best available professionals, in the hope of making some discoveries about the relationships of an audience to a play in performance and of actors to their profession. I was also entering a plea against over-intellectual and conceptual responses to Shakespeare. My knowledge of theatre practice led me to be provocative and speculative. And, yes, I did idealise actors for my purposes, as occasionally Charles Marowitz idealises directors. I would like to think our 'long-range goals' for theatre are more similar than this chapter of his book suggests.

John Russell Brown
September 1990

7 **Dab hands**

Shakespearian scholarship is the science-fiction of the intellectual classes. Like sci-fi, it regularly boards its flights of fancy and soars into the highest stratospheres of conjecture, regaling its readers with leaps of the imagination and elaborate excursions into fantasy. Unlike sci-fi, which does not seek to prove anything beyond its own fanciful inventions, Shakespearian scholarship is constantly validating its premises and propounding its arguments. It is none the less diverting for doing so, and indeed when it is most earnestly involved in 'proving' its points it is often at its most entertaining.

I do not question the fact that scholarship has unearthed many valuable insights into the works of the sixteenth and seventeenth centuries, and provided theatre practitioners with some convenient handles with which to hoist up many chunks of dramatic bric-à-brac. Indeed it could be argued that the styles now current at places such as the Royal Shakespeare Company and The National Theatre are direct descendants of the ideas and experiments of scholars such as William Poel and Harley Granville-Barker. The modern approach to Shakespearian acting would not exist if men such as these had not insisted on the faster tempi and commitment to meaning which they brought to their work in the early 1900s.

But in the past fifty or sixty years, the Shakespeare industry has turned into an academic Godzilla which rapaciously swallows up the Histories, the Tragedies and the Comedies and regularly disgorges a combination of steam and stool which passes for classical lore but is nothing more than the effluence of some raging academic incontinence. The majority of scholars, critics, theorists and analysts at work here ride the haunches of their extrapolations as if they were prize broncos – sometimes they stay on, sometimes they fall off, but the important thing is the tenacity of their ride and how many interesting flurries, flips, jerks and gyrations they can produce before being thrown to the ground. A recent copy of *The Shakespearian Quarterly*, published by the Folger Shakespeare Library, is a good example of the kind of dust they fling up. In this special issue, devoted to Shakespearian play criticism, only three of the sixteen articles display intellectual distinction, and another two or three just about pass muster. On the plus side, Ralph Berry's short, cogent piece, 'The Reviewer as Historian', deftly tries to define the critic's responsibility to be both chronicler and commentator. The late Bernard Beckerman, using Anthony Sher's *Richard III* and Georgio Strehler's *Tempest* as illustrations, urges the critic to transcend reportage and confront the 'illusion' that great productions often throw up. S. P. Cerasano, in 'Churls Just Wanna Have Fun', describes the convoluted chemistry that went into the creation of Sher's *Richard*, while Chris Hassell Jr breezily recapitulates the diverse critical reaction which sometimes defined and sometimes obscured that notable RSC production.

At the other extreme, close to the nadir of the volume, one finds Stephen Booth's woolly-minded 'The Shakespearian Actor as Kamikaze Pilot', a rambling 6000-word dissertation that merely makes the point that some of Shakespeare's characters are more focused and therefore more rewarding to play than others; and Mikel Lambert's 'Actors and Critics', which appears to be a thinly-veiled defence of the author's own critically ravaged productions. 'Shakespeare wrote plays, not literature. And plays are meant to be seen, not read', Lambert informs us. Her other perceptions are on a par with these staggering insights.

Another example of the pointlessness spawned by the industry is A. L. Rowse's latest tome, *Shakespeare's Self-portrait*, a short work which proceeds on the shaky assumption that, by culling sections from the Collected Works under headings such as Family, School, Love, Theatre, Places He Knew, etc., it is possible to build up a biographical portrait of the unbiographised W. S. This elaborate miscalculation produces a chrestomathy of Shakespearian excerpts which might nicely decorate the pages of a kitschy cultural calendar. The notion that what the playwright's characters have to say on these sundry subjects can or should be attributed to the playwright himself is as far-fetched as Rowse's other theories – like his allegedly incontestable assumption that Emilia Lanier was the Dark Lady of the sonnets. As a sample of Rowse's Rambo-like approach to scholarship, one must cite lines such as: 'since my discovery of who the Dark Lady was we can now appreciate what a remarkable personality hers was with whom the inflammable poet was infatuated. Shakespeare, in his open and free way, tells us everything about her except her name.' Now, thanks to Rowse, that too is revealed and, should you dare to question it, the author is prepared to bludgeon you to death with the weight of his considerable research. (I must, however, confess to a prejudice in the case of Rowse: anyone who has the fecklessness to dedicate his book 'to President Ronald Reagan for his historic honour to Shakespeare's profession' automatically renounces serious consideration. Anyone obtuse enough to find a connection between Ronald Reagan and 'Shakespeare's profession' is already, it seems to me, a reigning monarch in Cloud Cuckoo Land.)

For someone actively embroiled in the professional theatre, there is a kind of weird lunacy about a tract which explores the literary structure of a play as if that was the Rosetta Stone to its existential meaning. No doubt it satisfies an intellectual curiosity and, as a pursuit, is as diverting (and compulsive) as that of maniacs who live for crossword puzzles; but, because it has taken specialisation to such extremes, I begin to wonder if it serves any real purpose for people not subject to the same addiction.

I have read treatises which have studiously explored the number of times a particular noun has recurred in a Shakespearian play, investing that recurrence with profound significance; how the use of capital letters was a guide to Elizabethan understanding; how printing and punctuation contained tell-tale hints about the author's secret meaning; how the existence of a particular historical character at a particular time in history was 'the key' to understanding the veiled significance of a particular play. The complexity of the theories is mind-boggling, the breadth of discoveries breathtaking. The fact that there is perpetual discord among the theorists and discoverers is somehow taken to be a sign of scholarship's salutary democratic air. Everyone, it seems to say, is entitled to be as idiosyncratic or hare-brained as everyone else. Sometimes I envisage Shakespearian scholarship as a cozy suburban sanatorium, in which lovably dotty people regale each other with an endless store of inexhaustible anecdotes and ever-changing personae. One day an inmate is Napoleon, the next, Alexander the Great, the day after that, Marie Antoinette – and so forth and so on, to the general amusement of inmates, staff and guests: a kind of rarefied Bedlam where only the over-educated, the remorselessly cerebral and the incorrigibly eccentric are admitted.

The academic insight is the apogee of academic inquiry, and it is a game not unlike that played by very bad actors: the ones who can sit around a table for hours and theorise a performance so enthrallingly that it is difficult to appreciate how bad they really are – until, of course, they get on their feet and demonstrate their ideas. The professors never have to get on their feet at all. Their theories may be countered by other professors, although they are just as likely to be seconded and extolled. But since they exist merely as theories, they never have to worry about being conclusively disproven. How do you conclusively disprove something which, in the realm of conjecture, can never be conclusively proven? An actor or director, on the other hand, tests his theories before audiences, and they not only *can* be proven, they are *obliged* to be – and when they are not, they suffer humiliation and disgrace. But, no matter how misguided their ideas may be, they always exist in a pragmatic framework predicated on the performance of a writer's work. They may be tried and found wanting, but they are always tried. Indeed, trial and error is the *modus operandi* of these theories, and, because it is, actors learn to sift valid information out of fallacious ideas and distinguish as they would put it, good choices from bad.

The academic is as good as his or her powers of critical persuasion, which means that bad thinkers who are good writers often appear to carry the day. Who is to gainsay them? Only other academics better versed in argument, polemic and supposition. Often what they are proving is not only unverifiable – no matter how many arguments they marshal – but irrelevant to the meaning of the plays. Which does not mean irrelevant to scholarship, for it is one of the great anomalies of this profession that something can be valuable to scholarship, even when it is utterly worthless to anyone else. Its value exists on a kind of imaginative level – like pornography – where orgasm can take place in the privacy of one's own room with reference only to an illusory sex-object which need not exist at all – except in the mind of the masturbator.

Intellectually speaking, when we say someone is 'wanking' we usually mean he is indulging in personal ratiocination without direct reference to the subject at hand (no pun intended). 'Wanking' implies working up a quantity of useful energy and then squandering it on personal satisfaction which, pleasurable as it may be to the wanker, does not fertilise any seed or benefit anyone else.

In Academe, wanking is a full-time job, and teaching others how to wank, a sign of intellectual respectability. The yardstick of successful wanking, if you are a professor or lecturer, is the number of periodicals which will allow you to wank for them in public; if you are a critic, the number of books devoted to wanking which will be circulated to other members of the cult, and the amount of notoriety your wanks will incite – compared to the wanks of older and more knowledgeable hands. The crowning success of a wanker is not so much to have his wanks bound and circulated but to transfer them into the minds of non-wankers (directors) who are dealing practically with material which the wanker deals with only pornographically. In short, the wanker who manages to drop his seed onto fertile ground in order to test the validity of his wanks has automatically transcended wanking altogether and is now in the realm of Real Life. Now, his theories must be either validated or nullified – and, because this is a prospect as daunting as it is tantalising, the majority of wankers prefer to wank in private, and never wander into the public arena.

Invidious as this may sound, I acknowledge that there is good scholarship and there is bad scholarship, and it is wrong to lump them all together, but what I do impugn is the tendency of writers to examine the most abstruse aspects of scholarly questions in a spirit of audacious inquiry, without realising that they are splitting hairs and vivisecting follicles. How essential is it, ultimately, to trace the number of times 'conscience' occurs in *Hamlet* or 'nuncle' in *King Lear*? Can a computerised, grossly mechanistic view of the plays really yield startling insights or is it something that scholars have fallen into because all the more obvious issues have already been thoroughly dealt with? Can there be a valid scholarship without a genuine, intuitive grasp of theatrical art? Can one divorce the Quarto and Folio texts from their existential impact in a theatre? And if not, can minute probing of the verse and its literary implications have real pertinence outside the realities of stage-performance? Have we reached a stage where scholars are simply talking to scholars in the way that computers talk to other computers, with all the rest of us wondering what all that buzzing, droning and bleeping is really all about?

Seeds of 'Verfremdung' in A Midsummer Night's Dream

The instructions contained in Hamlet's advice to the players are often quoted as a credo for theatrical realism and there are many classical actors who find in its precepts the touchstone of their art. But it may be worth pointing out that there is an entirely complementary aesthetic contained in III.i of *A Midsummer Night's Dream* which can serve just as readily as a basis for surrealism, symbolism and even Epic Theatre. This is the scene in which the mechanicals proceed to rehearse *Pyramus and Thisbe*, a parody of a classic tale which, ironically, can be seen as a harbinger of all the Shakespearian parodies that were to proliferate in the late eighteenth and nineteenth centuries.

'There are things in this comedy of Pyramus and Thisbe', says Bottom 'that will never please. First, Pyramus must draw a sword to kill himself, which the ladies cannot abide. How answer you that?' And when they speak of leaving out the killing, Bottom comes up with a perfect stylistic solution: 'Write me a prologue', he says, 'and let the prologue seem to say, we will do no harm with our swords, and that Pyramus is not killed indeed, and for the more better assurance, tell them that I, Pyramus, am not Pyramus, but Bottom the weaver; this will put them out of fear.' Three hundred years before the advent of Erwin Piscator or Bertolt Brecht, Bottom hits upon a device to 'alienate' his performance, removing from it any shred of verisimilitude. For, as soon as the audience have been made aware of the acting devices to be incorporated in the play, they will no longer respond to them viscerally, but view them with the same kind of objectivity that Brecht himself sought to achieve at the Berliner Ensemble. By producing an overview of the action which removes its tendency to frighten or involve, Peter Quince and his troupe prevent the audience from being 'carried away' or put in the grips of emotions which cloud their reason and blind them to the play's larger implications.

When Snout raises the problem that the ladies might be affrighted by the sight of a lion, Bottom, again with a budding Brechtian percipience, offers another non-naturalistic solution. 'Nay, you must name his name,' says Bottom (dislocating the theatrical illusion from the social reality which underpins it) 'and half his face must be seen through the lion's neck; and he himself must speak through, saying thus, or to the same defect: "Ladies" or "Fair ladies" "I would wish you" or "I would request you" or "I would entreat you not to fear, not to tremble; my life for yours. If you think I come hither as a lion, it were pity of my life: no, I am no such thing: I am a man as other men are" and there indeed let him name his name, and tell them plainly he is Snug the joiner.'

In short, let there be a stylistic suggestion of 'lion' in the lion's head itself, but destroy its illusion by revealing the actor underneath, thereby drawing attention simultaneously to both the reality and the illusion. Alienate the whole idea of a 'wild animal' by forcing the audience to discriminate between the illusion and the nullifying anti-illusionary device. And, what is more, with this device affirm the common humanity that exists between the performers and the public. A telling example of Shakespeare's innate populist sympathies – that same tendency which we can discern in so many of the plays where the author instinctively identifies himself with the teeming, Elizabethan multitude of which he is only a part. 'A man' indeed '*as other men are*' (my italics).

But there are even more brilliant touches of *Verfremdung* still to come. For, when the actors concede that it is virtually impossible to bring moonlight onto the stage, Peter Quince suggests: '. . . one must come in with a bush of thorns and a lanthorn, and say he comes to disfigure, or to present of Moonshine'. With the deft appropriation of two unrelated props, a clump of thorns to represent the distant foliage and a simple lantern to represent the light of the moon behind it, Shakespeare has succeeded in creating a striking visual symbol – not unlike the sparse, highly economical imagery that Teo Otto brought to the production of *Mother Courage* where, needing to suggest a wagon in motion, he hit upon the brilliant notion of actually using a wagon which, with the use of a revolve, could actually be put into motion. A contemporary refinement of devices originally created by Shakespeare for the primitive but evocative settings of the Elizabethan stage.

But the most brilliant of all Shakespeare's stylistic inventions is seen when his actors are obliged to solve the problem of creating a wall and a chink through which the lovers must speak. 'Some man or other must present Wall', says Bottom, plunging into the art of symbolic representation three centuries before the advent of Maeterlinck or Alexander Blok, 'and let him have some plaster, or some loam, or some rough-cast about him, to signify wall' and let him hold his fingers thus, and through that cranny shall Pyramus and Thisbe whisper.'

A few dabs of texture, and a thumb pressed against the index finger to create an aperture and, at one stroke, Shakespeare has created a fetching piece of surrealist stagecraft through which Pyramus may consort with Thisbe at Ninus' tomb. And what are the minimalist choices of contemporary directors such as Bertolt Brecht, Jerzy Grotowski or Peter Brook but contemporary ramifications of those primitive symbolic devices first proffered by Shakespeare in a playlet which was itself a minimalisation of one of the great antique legends inherited by the Elizabethan age?

In the mechanicals' version of *Pyramus and Thisbe*, as in Brecht's theory of *Verfremdung* the object is to create a distanced perspective through which the social implications of the action can be glimpsed without an audience 'losing itself' in emotions which might otherwise obscure those insights. Through the devices of Bottom, Peter Quince and the rest of his players, Shakespeare enables us to see the vast differences of class and artistic perception which existed between simple Elizabethan workers and the bourgeois members of the court. Even as we laugh at the rough-hewn charades of the mechanicals, we become aware that their derision by Theseus, Hippolyta, Lysander and Demetrius is sowing the seeds of that social upheaval which, in England, was only half-a-century away and which, when it came, would totally reverse the *Weltanschauung* and make us look at plays like *A Midsummer Night's Dream* in a completely different light.

(The above specimen of Shakespearian analysis, or versions equally absurd, can be found in learned journals on both sides of the Atlantic. It is almost impossible to satirise them because the Real McCoys are much more breathtaking in their sophistry than anything a satirist might conjure up.)

The Shakespearian fallacies of John Barton

8

John Barton is as old as the Royal Shakespeare Company – a bit older in fact. He has been connected with it since 1960 and has served as an Associate Director since 1964. He has directed close to thirty productions and, for over three decades, has been a pervasive influence on its acting company. He was brought into the organisation by its founder Peter Hall, functioned regularly throughout the reign of Trevor Nunn and remained ensconced under the recent regime of director Terry Hands. A Cambridge don and a recognised authority on Shakespeare, Barton has been the single greatest influence on English verse-speaking for three generations of British actors.

In 1984, in association with London Weekend Television, Barton created a nine-part series on the subject of Shakespearian acting. In the same year, Methuen published *Playing Shakespeare*, which was, essentially, the record of those programmes, compiled in book form. In it, one gets a chance to consider John Barton's ideas about Shakespearian acting first hand and how those ideas have influenced his productions and the work of those actors with whom he has come into contact. In doing so, one learns a great deal about both the splendours and the inadequacies of Shakespearian production in England.

The basic assumption behind Barton's approach is that, if one can find the proper clues, Shakespeare himself instructs the actor on how to perform the plays. The structure of the verse, the implied stresses, the use of enjambement and elision are all there to guide the actor towards the author's meaning.

But, to believe this, one also has to believe that Shakespeare, in the full flush of inspiration, was simultaneously constructing signposts and inserting technical indications to his actors. Anyone who understands how a playwright's mind works, assuming of course he is a talented playwright and not a bloodless craftsman, knows this is nonsense. There are certain obvious indications of intent in all writing, as there is in Shakespeare, and Barton refers to them: short or broken lines usually indicate rapid delivery; a caesura provides a natural break; enjambement encourages a confluence between thoughts and militates against end-stopping, etc., etc. All of this is incontestable, in the same way that punctuation (whether Shakespeare's or the printer's) is a fairly straightforward indicator of breaths, pauses, upward and downward inflections. But to assume that Shakespeare 'built in' acting instructions which the actor can deduce from the structure of the verse is to be blind to the thousand and one permutations of which every line is capable when run through the strainer of an actor's sensibility. Also it suggests a degree of consciousness which is antithetical to the organic (that is, unconscious) flow that runs beneath a work of art. The 'sense' that Barton and his collaborators pursue is never a 'given' – for that is the fruit of the actor's art, not the playwright's. The dogma of an actor's interpretation is able to trample every self-evident law of prosody and triumph in ways which neither the author nor the scholar could ever imagine.

To believe as Barton does that the rhythm of a speech resides in the verse like the nut in the nutshell is to misunderstand the function of rhythm in the actor's work. Tempo marks such as 'slow', 'fast', 'crescendo' or 'decrescendo' have a certain formal significance in music, but not in verse. The nature of an actor's idea can successfully retard even the most obviously nimble verse passage, just as a novel or unexpected idea can accelerate what, from the academic point of view, appears to be a slow section weighted with caesuras. The problem here, and it is apparent throughout Barton's commentary to his actors, is that the director does not understand the Stanislavskian meaning of words such as 'action' (that is, intention) and 'beat' (unit of purpose) and the ways in which interpretative choices can transform the written word. To put it bluntly, although he knows a great deal about prosody, Barton in my view knows virtually nothing about acting.

Discussing the Trial Scene in *The Merchant of Venice*, one hears Barton hammering away at his thesis. 'Here again, I believe Shakespeare is giving hidden stage-directions to the actor. When there is a short line, we can be pretty sure that he is indicating a pause of some sort.'

SHYLOCK	O wise and upright judge!
	How much more elder art thou than thy looks!
PORTIA	Therefore lay bare your bosom.
SHYLOCK	Ay, his breast.
	So say the bond, doth it not, noble judge?
	'Nearest his heart': those are the very words.
PORTIA	It is so.
	Are there balance here to weigh the flesh?
SHYLOCK	I have them ready.
PORTIA	Have by some surgeon, Shylock, on your charge,
	To stop his wounds lest he do bleed to death.

'I've said that a short line in Shakespeare usually suggests a pause', says Barton, 'and is some sort of hint to an actor about how to play a scene'. And proceeding on tht assumption, Barton suggests: 'after [Portia's] short line "It is so", she pauses so that she and the court shall take in the gravity of the situation.' 'That's right', answers actor David Suchet 'and Shylock, because of his emotional state and his confidence, is in no doubt about what he's doing here and comes bang in with each speech'. 'So it is Portia', resumes Barton, 'who has the pauses because she is weighing Shylock up and deciding how to handle him. When she pauses after he has said he has the scales ready, the pause marks her disgust at his eagerness, and she weights her words before she goes on. So we can see how Shakespeare's short lines can always tell us something, usually about the character's intentions.'

All of which sounds eminently sensible until one regards the scene from a dramatic standpoint and finds that the real 'climax' of the exchange comes in Shylock's next speech:

SHYLOCK	Is it so nominated in the bond?
PORTIA	It is not so expressed, but what of that?
	'Twere good you do so much for charity.
SHYLOCK	I cannot find it; 'tis not in the bond.

If that *is* zinger in the scene – the realisation that Shylock will not make the slightest move towards mitigating his cruel purpose – then the best way to arrive at it is to have a fluent, continuous exchange from 'O wise and upright Judge' right up to Shylock's: 'Is it so nominated in the bond?' Pauses along the way, such as those suggested for Portia, merely subvert the *significant* pause before Shylock's line ('I cannot find it; 'tis not in the bond') when his hard-heartedness effectively stymies Portia's drive towards charity. Shakespeare may have had 'pauses' in mind when he wrote short lines, and a pause after 'It is so' may have been a useful device in the nineteenth century for the court 'to take in the gravity of the situation', but, if actors and director are looking for the more telling moment, it makes better sense to roll directly to that point when Shylock's mercilessness is most nakedly revealed. Again, I do not propose this merely as an 'alternative choice' but to illustrate that Barton's method, based on an arcane understanding of Shakespeare's original intentions, tends to sacrifice dramatic effect for some woolly-minded principle of poetic rectitude.

Not content to impute built-in meaning to the verse, Barton extends the theory to Shakespeare's prose, ever hoping to find stress and sense copulating together. Barton turns to Mercutio's speech in *Romeo and Juliet* just as the character has been wounded.

MERCUTIO: No, 'tis not so deep as a well, nor so wide as a church door. But 'tis enough. 'T'will serve. Ask for me tomorrow, and you shall find me a grave man. I am peppered, I warrant, for this world. A plague a' both your houses! Zounds, a dog, a rat, a mouse, a cat, to scratch a man to death! A braggart, a rogue, a villain, that fights by the book of arithmetic! Why the devil came you between us? I was hurt under your arm.

ROMEO: I thought all for the best.

MERCUTIO: Help me into some house, Benvolio, or I shall faint. A plague a' both your houses! They have made worms' meat of me. I have it, and soundly too. Your houses!

'I would argue', says Barton, 'that there are six strong stresses in the last seven words. "You-shall-find-me-a-grave-man" – seven slow monosyllables, slow as monosyllabic lines usually are in Shakespeare. It is a good rhythm for Mercutio here who is sardonic, self-mocking and tough.'

But Mercutio, whose character may be said to have been 'sardonic, self-mocking and tough', is none of these things in the present situation – injured by a wound which will shortly prove fatal. His 'action' in the Stanislavsky sense may be 'to tough out a pose reconcilable with his established persona', or 'to convince Romeo and the others that he is in a much more serious condition than they believe'. Or, it may be as simple a physical action as trying to muster the breath necessary to convey his shock at having been wounded. In any of the former readings, the rendering of 'seven slow monosyllables' would go right against the actor's choice. It is just as conceivable that, trying to draw breath with difficulty, his words coming out in a jumble, the actor might opt for one stress: 'Ask-for-me-*tomorrow* and you-shall-find-me-a-grave-man.' Or, playing against the obvious rendering of the line and recognising the wound as mortal (and therefore no longer 'sardonic or self-mocking') – 'Ask for me tomorrow [pause, then quietly as a swallowed line trailing off into inaudibility] and-you-shall-find-me-a-grave-man.'

What Barton's seven syllabic stresses convey is merely the most obvious reading of the line – the one that custom has burned into our minds. Again, the trap is that by looking in the verse for what should be brought to it, Barton uncovers literary rather than dramatic meaning.

Barton then draws a comparison between Brutus's speech to the Roman populace and that of Mark Antony:

BRUTUS: Romans, countrymen and lovers, hear me for my cause, and be silent, that you may hear. Believe me for mine honour, and have respect to mine honour, that you may believe. Censure me in your wisdom, and awake your senses, that you may the better judge. If there be any in this assembly, any dear friend of Caesar's, to him I say that Brutus' love to Caesar was no less than his. If then that friend demand why Brutus rose against Caesar, this is my answer: Not that I loved Caesar less, but that I loved Rome more. Had you rather Caesar were living, and die all slaves, than that Caesar were dead, to live all free men? As Caesar loved me, I weep for him; as he was fortunate, I rejoice at it; as he was valiant, I honour him; but, as he was ambitious, I slew him. There is tears for his love; joy for his fortune; honour for his valour, and death for his ambition. Who is here so base that would be a bondman? If any, speak; for him have I offended. Who is here so vile that will not love his country? If any, speak; for him have I offended. I pause for a reply.

Barton's verdict on this speech, assisted by remarks from actor Ben Kingsley, is that it is 'studied and not spontaneous ... The antitheses are so laboured that it all sounds prepared, as if Brutus conned it in the study in front of his mirror. So it's a deliberate contrast to the easy, more natural arguments of Antony.'

ANTONY: Friends, Romans, countrymen, lend me your ears;
I come to bury Caesar, not to praise him.
The evil that men do lives after them,
The good is oft interred with their bones;
So let it be with Caesar. The noble Brutus
Hath told you Caesar was ambitious,
If it were so, it was a grievous fault,
And grievously hath Caesar answered it.
Here, under leave of Brutus and the rest –
For Brutus is an honourable man;
So are they all, all honourable men –
Come I to speak in Caesar's funeral.
He was my friend, faithful and just to me;
But Brutus says he was ambitious,
And Brutus is an honourable man,
He hath brought many captives home to Rome,
Whose ransoms did the general coffers fill;
When that the poor have cried, Caesar hath wept;
Ambition should be made of sterner stuff.
Yet Brutus says he was ambitious,
And Brutus is an honourable man.

Barton suggests that Antony 'very cleverly decides to undercut Brutus' speech by being simple and direct' – whereas Brutus was 'rhetorical and pompous' – but if that is the case why has Shakespeare given Brutus prose and Mark Antony verse? Is it just conceivable that Shakespeare intends the reverse – for Brutus, who is genuinely in two minds about the assassination, to be simple and direct, sincerely trying to justify the act both to himself and the crowd, and Antony 'rhetorical' and 'pompous' because he realises he has to eradicate Brutus's sincerity and rouse the populace to revenge?

I would not be so bold as to say which tack is correct because, clearly, there are dozens of different ways of approaching each character's speech, but if I am to be guided by something resembling human psychology, I, as Brutus, could well use that speech as a public correlative for private ambivalence, or, to put it more simply: to try to justify both to myself and others why I felt it necessary to take Caesar's life; my 'action' being to try to construct a generalisation with which I could continue to live in the face of that dastardly crime. The grounds for Mark Antony's 'actions' are much more clearly focused in the play. They are referred to in his speech to Brutus directly after the assassination:

> I know not gentlemen, what you intend,
> Who else must be let blood, who else is rank:
> If I myself, there is no hour so fit
> As Caesar's death's hour; nor no instrument
> Of half that worth as those your swords, made rich
> With the most noble blood of all this world.

Antony has to create a protective shield around himself by impunging Brutus's motives and fostering a moral condemnation which will turn the crowd against the assassins. At the same time, he needs to plant the seeds for a re-evaluation of the murder itself. To do this, he may well have recourse to 'rhetoric' and a highly dramatic form of delivery. Having been Caesar's friend, he is himself in mortal danger from the conspirators. His only defence against his own possible assassination is the sympathy of the crowd. His own skin is at stake and this may well justify a certain pressure behind his oratory. No matter how simply he may begin, he has a vested interest in turning the crowd against the crime and its perpetrators. The key to the character's speech is not to be found in theories of 'rhetoric' or 'naturalism', but in personal actions consistent with the established character and growing out of the stresses of the situation. Again, we see that Barton's 'reasonable' reading of Shakespeare's words can be turned topsy-turvy, simply by re-angling the motives of one character or the other.

Another of Barton's fanciful ideas concerns the soliloquy – whether it should be 'done to oneself' or 'shared with the audience'. 'There are very few absolute rules with Shakespeare', says Barton, clearing the decks for the assertion of one, 'but I personally believe that it's right, 99 times out of a hundred, to share a soliloquy with the audience. I'm convinced it's a grave distortion of Shakespeare's intention to do it to oneself. If the actor shares the speech it will work. If he doesn't, it will be dissipated and the audience won't listen properly.'

To prove this theory, Barton asks Jane Lapotaire, looking at herself in the mirror, to try a speech of Cressida's:

CRESSIDA: Words, vows, gifts, tears and love's full sacrifice,
  He offers in another's enterprise;
  But more in Troilus thousandfold I see

> Than in the glass of Pandar's praise may be.
> Yet hold I off: women are angels, wooing
> Things won are done – joy's soul lies in the doing ...

Barton then leaps in to opine: 'For the first line or two, we got interested in Cressida's vanity and her self-absorption, but when Jane went on playing the same thing, the speech didn't go anywhere and got stuck. It became a generalized comment on her vanity rather than an invitation to us to listen and to share her thoughts.'

Barton's notion that for a speech to be effectively played and 'shared with the audience' it has to be *directed* to them stems from a shortsightedness common among British directors about engendering private moods in public situations. The notion that the only way to 'share' a speech with an audience is to play it to them flies in the face of approximately ninety years of Stanislavskian research which found that, if the actor's personal mood is properly centred and sustained, it encourages the audience to 'come to him' and, by doing so, to see into his private meditation, maintaining the integrity of his character and the play's given circumstances. It preserves the aesthetic assumption that a soliloquy is not happening in a theatre but in a socio-psychological ambience in which the audience, paradoxically, is privy to a character's private thoughts.

It was because soliloquies were such a strain on credibility that Chekhov eventually eliminated them from his plays and they became, for good or ill, a convention associated with 'the bad old days' of the Russian theatre. Now, in Shakespeare during the nineteenth century, soliloquies *were* shared with the audience, projected as histrionic set pieces in order to have a one-to-one impact with the public. There is no question that direct address to the audience can be theatrically effective, just as being assaulted on the street by a total stranger forces you to relate to someone who has suddenly decided to relate to you, but it is the more obvious of the two approaches to soliloquies. And the idea that direct address to the audience 'shares a character's thoughts' more effectively than the subjective approach is wholly specious.

The real question is to whom the character is addressing himself when he begins to speak his thoughts alone on stage – to the audience? to some delicate receptivity in his inner being? to his divided self? to a past self? to a memory of a recent event? to a paradox in his own character? The Chorus in *Henry V* is clearly talking to the audience and asking it to compensate, with its imagination, for the poverty of Elizabethan stage settings, it would be nonsense to play that as a 'private moment', but Cressida is not directing her thoughts to a multifarious group of spectators in Stratford-upon-Avon but to a notion engendered from Pandarus's speech; the notion that, if too quickly won, she will not be sufficiently appreciated.

Barton urges Michael Pennington, trying Hamlet's soliloquy, to reverse his personal meditation and 'share it with us', 'take us with you', and when the actor, from Barton's standpoint, achieves this, he declares approvingly: 'He didn't come on and issue a statement about his state of mind. He opened himself to us and worked it out with us. It doesn't work', insists Barton 'if the audience stands back and observes the character thinking. The actor must open himself to his audience and make them think with him because he needs to share his problems. In dialogue a character reaches out to another character and in a soliloquy a character reaches out to the audience. There's no great difference between the two.'

But, of course, there is a world of difference between the two! In the former, the character's 'reaching out' to another character forges a unit of subjective contact which, when plausible and organic, invites the objective attentions of the audience. *We* are drawn in because *they* are drawn in. *We* believe because *they* believe. The reverse, as we well know from bad performances, is equally true. When characters do not make contact with one another, when their centre is in the auditorium rather than the situation in which they allegedly find themselves, our interest wanes and we become aware of 'acting' *per se*. There is no plausible illusion and, hence, nothing in which to believe. In a soliloquy, unless the actor has transformed the public into another character (Henry V in the St Crispin's Day speech addressing us as his army or Mark Antony orating to the audience as if it were the Roman populace, etc.), direct assault on the audience's perceptions denies the previously maintained fiction of the play's given circumstances. If Hamlet is 'working out with us' philosophical contradictions concerning the futility of life, the soliloquy is in danger of becoming a discourse on a subject which, because it is directed to us, suggests we have some personal stake in it. But we do not. Hamlet's dilemma is peculiar to himself. It grows out of his stressful circumstances. It may have a bearing of our views of similar matters but we have not come to the theatre to 'share' *those*. We have come to consider *his*. On a subconscious level, we understand that a profound consideration of his dilemmas pertains to ours, but not *immediately*, not at the very moment we are making the imaginative effort to enter into *his* thoughts and *his* circumstance. If Hamlet's words have any kind of historical or artistic credibility, they can only engage us subjectively – by engendering our empathy and making us feel his turmoils and conflicts. That is best served by creating such a palpable sense of the character's otherness that we, the audience, are sucked into his world. To be forcibly reminded of our own, although it produces a momentary theatrical *frisson*, cannot help but emphasise the contrived nature of his. By incorporating the audience, the character automatically renounces the disbelief which we have willingly suspended for his sake. What an audience has come to 'share' is not the piecemeal thoughts of a character in a set monologue, but the larger vision of the world in which that character operates. It is Shakespeare who has created the pretext for that 'sharing' and the actor's job is to maintain it for the author's sake. To rationalise its abdication on the grounds that certain parts of it should be sliced out of context and arbitrarily 'shared with the audience' is a violation of the pact that all actors enter into when they agree to appear in a play; namely, to conjure up the actions and perceptions of fictitious persons. It is a misconception of the 'aesthetic contract' which, in the theatre, takes precedence over any 'social contract' which may be loosely negotiated between the actor and his public.

Because he is a Cambridge don and a man enamoured of language, the linguistic impulse is always foremost with Barton; however it is not the most essential factor in shaping a performance. At one point, having described Philo's speech in *Antony and Cleopatra* as 'choric', he asks Ben Kingsley to perform it, so as to deliver its information. This done, actress Lisa Harrow points out that Philo, despite the fact that he furnishes us with information about Antony's weakness for Cleopatra, is nevertheless a character and it is his character's *attitude* which colours the speech – with which Barton agrees: 'Yes, you're absolutely right. I'm cheating if I just say it's "choric". What I am really saying is "Make the language your first concern."' He then encourages Ben Kingsley to take a running jump at the speech, so as to be outraged 'at what you've just seen'. Barton's conclusion: 'Good, the language made you angry. We did have an interesting thing

there, didn't we? We worked the wrong way round. We started
with the language and then went to the intentions . . . occasionally,
it's valuable to start with the text and the language only.'

But it is the formation of character and that character's
conception of his wants which determine the rhythm and colour
of the language. There is virtually no way an actor can 'start with
the language' and, as it were, add intention and the semblance of
character. It is quite thumpingly 'the wrong way round'! Language is the end-product of intention and desire. It is because we
want something and try to satisfy our desires in obtaining it that
we speak at all. A baby without desire or intention is normally
passive. It is when hunger or cold or fear stimulates the baby into
action that it begins to make sounds, that it looks for language to
satisfy its desires or mitigate its pain. It may be academically
useful for Barton to point out that 'antithesis is a common factor
in Shakespearian language' (although this is true of most Elizabethan writing and is in no way peculiar to Shakespeare) and it
may be instructive to show actors how certain words and phrases
pit themselves against each other in order to produce a counter-
point, but an 'antithesis' in itself is merely a piece of literary
brickwork. Until one has established the thrust of the scene, the
'want' of the character and the obstacles being posed by his
fellow-characters, there is no indication as to how to express that
language. It is not to the rules of prosody nor the theories of verse
structure that an actor must look in order to find the meaning
with which to transfuse Shakespeare's words; that is forked out of
the crucible in which his instinct and imagination swirl together.
And to suggest that a speech, a character or an entire play can be
'decoded' by understanding its prosody or its semiology is grossly
to misunderstand the nature of theatrical performance.

Throughout Barton's 'advice to the actors', one is constantly
coming across metaphorical descriptions of what acting is;
similes and metaphors which describe results rather than elabor-
ations of the techniques which produce those results. 'Imagine
the text is a ball and your wits are like two rackets. One of you
serves the ball up and the other hits it back as hard as he can. It's
a rally and one of you is going to ace the other at the end. By
making it a tennis-match, you can make me sit up, and live
through it with you.'

All of this smacks of the worst aspects of British amateurism –
jolly bursts of fetching imagery which are supposed to inspire 'the
lads and lasses' to 'have a bash'. It is the antithesis of rooted

technique and makes a mockery of over a century of acting theory from Stanislavsky, to Michael Chekhov, to Brecht to Artaud. But, worse than all of this, it serves no practical purpose. It is not a metaphor that illustrates an aesthetic or theoretical principle, a simplification of a more profound idea. It is a merely a gauche attempt to 'describe' results which more astute intelligences realise can only come about from applied theories which deal with the basic chemistry of acting: action-playing, psychology of character, and the mastery of inner technique.

Because Barton's preoccupations are essentially academic, the whole notion of a production concept is alien to his work. His role, as he sees it, is to help the actor unlock the secrets of Shakespearian text and, once this is done, it is for the actor to characterise as he sees fit: '... though the conception of a production may be mine, the actual performance is something that in a deep sense no longer really belongs to me. So though I may have strong views about how Shakespeare saw Shylock, these views were rightly transformed by Patrick [Stewart] and David [Suchet]. Their rich performances are therefore theirs more than mine. And that I think is how it should be.'

A 'directorial conception' postulates a slate of characterisations which elucidate and reinforce an *a priori* attitude to the material. If actors' performances remain independent of such a conception, it suggests a directorial framework so flexible as to be non-existent. But then, if a production concept is restricted to the textual interpretation of individual speeches, the term is a misnomer anyway. A conception is a way of seeing a classic and it implies a particularity of vision which necessitates character delineation along one line and not another. If there are no parameters concerning what actors can do with their roles, the director is effectively renouncing a personal interpretation. It is common in England for directors to encourage and coax performances out of their cast and then assemble them into a 'production pattern', but that approach must be distinguished from the work of directors who come to a play with an overriding idea of its intellectual meaning and accompanying visual imagery. For such a director, the cast is 'free' only in so much as their freedom coincides with the larger intentions of the *mise-en-scène*. If, as Barton suggests, the actors are *entitled* to their own characterisations and owe no allegiance to a directorial overview, we are in an area of play production very far from the practice of a Peter Brook, a Peter Stein, a Roger Planchon or a Lyubimov.

I do not want to suggest that Barton is either a fraud or a charlatan, nor that he is consistently off-base. He is a resourceful scholar and he knows more about the nuances of blank verse than most directors working in England. And when he talks about the actor's need to 'relish the words' in prose as well as in verse, he is putting his finger on a very real difference between British and American acting. The Americans feel that the words themselves will do them service; the British actor knows the words need to be propelled and enriched with resonant sound and forceful articulation in order to soar across the footlights. But when Barton finds stress and pretends he is simultaneously uncovering meaning, he is falling helplessly into academic quicksand. There is 'obvious' stress in almost all of Shakespeare's verse and it does not take an actor from the Royal Shakespeare Company to find it. But the notion that stress is built-in and methodically extractable is a recipe for the dullest kind of Shakespearian elocution. Stress is not an attribute of prosody but a by-product of intention, and only when an actor's objectives have been formulated out of personal choices about character and situation will dramatic sense ensue. And there, perhaps, is the main difference between Barton's logic and my own. For him, making sense out the poetry automatically brings sense to the performance, whereas most seasoned actors know that dramatic sense evolves not from verbal analysis but from judicious selection – through trial and error – of appropriate actions; that is, meanings brought to the text by the actor through the director's intercession and derived from his larger conception of where those words belong in the universe of the play. It is this which shapes the verse afresh and literally gives us 'new' meanings in what Shakespeare has written.

Brook's shifting-
9 point

When I first arrived in England in the early sixties one of my most refreshing and, in retrospect, fertilising experiences was my encounter with Peter Brook. We had written for the same theatre publication, *Encore Magazine*, and gradually got to know each other – so much so that we agreed to collaborate on a theatrical project – although 'collaboration' is far too active a word to describe that first association at the Royal Shakespeare Company in 1964 when I acted as a kind of aesthetic kibitzer and 'noises off' on the Paul Scofield *King Lear*. I was struck forcibly by the airborne quality of Peter's imagination and the remorselessness with which he sought production-results. I was also struck by the overriding seriousness with which everyone at the RSC treated their work. Although there was as much levity and horseplay as one finds in any theatrical milieu, underlying the pranks and badinage was a palpable conviction that Shakespeare was important *and* difficult and demanding of one's most strenuous efforts.

Over the years, I have taken exception to several of Peter's productions and written some close-to-the-knuckle reviews which undoubtedly put a strain on our relationship, but I have never failed to admire his inventiveness, his audacity and his unquenchable tendency to *go beyond* – not only himself but the conventional practice of his contemporaries. Despite differences of opinion, some of which verged upon the ideological, I have always felt we were pursuing the theatre in a similar frame of mind and proceeding from a set of shared values in regard to politics, aesthetics and classics.

In *The Shifting Point*, a collection of sundry writings from about thirty years of Peter's work in the theatre, there is a short essay entitled 'What is a Shakespeare? which gave me a rather serious jolt. The piece defines Shakespeare as being different not only in 'quality', but in 'kind' and traces Brook's view on Shake-spearian production from his very earliest productions to the present.

After describing the ways by which directors – himself in-cluded – approach certain works from the standpoint of 'per-sonal' expression, that is, mounting highly individualised 'inter-pretations' of the plays, he concludes that: 'What [Shakespeare] wrote is not interpretation; it is the thing itself.' Shakespeare's work, according to Brook, is not merely 'Shakespeare's view of the world, it's something which actually resembles reality.' By which I take it he means that, whereas we may all have impressions and interpretations *based* on Shakespeare, what makes all those multifarious views possible is the work itself, which constitutes some kind of wide, variegated, endless resource like the given phenomena of the natural world. The canon in Peter's view should be viewed as 'an enormous skein of inter-related words' which makes up a highly rich 'fabric' from which audiences receive innumerable impulses – rather than pre-ordained author's 'messages' which individual sensibilities (directors) diminish into personalised statements which, in any case, 'can never be complete'. One must always realise, says Brook, that 'subjective versions of the play', no matter how affecting, may often be 'less than the play itself'.

When Brook first began working on Shakespeare, he himself proceeded along these subjective lines, providing his personal view of *Love's Labour's Lost*, *Coriolanus* and so on, creating per-sonal imagery through which his view of the plays could be ex-pressed. However, says Brook, 'Since then, my view has changed, evolved, through a growing awareness that the overall unifying image was much less than the play itself ... that a production of Shakespeare could go beyond the unity that one man's imagina-tion could give, beyond that of the director and the designer.' The new impetus, says Brook, 'starts always with the instinctive feeling that the play needs to be done, now': that it has become pertinent or relevant to artists and public because of a coinci-dence between the work and certain immediate social, spiritual or political circumstances. Brook concludes that it is not enough simply to present a public with the artistic proofs of a director's desire to do a certain play because 'as long as one's in the first instinct, "I like this, I want to do it", one is most likely within the closed circle of wishing to illustrate what one likes: "I like it, and I'll show you why I like it". The next step is, "I like it, because it parallels all that I need to know about the world." ... Personal expression ceases to be an aim and we go toward shared discovery.'

When I was director of The Open Space in London, in various interviews I was often asked what my 'theatrical aim' was – the assumption always being that a director obviously had a 'theatrical aim' and, having it, there was no reason in the world why it could not be clearly articulated. I often found myself answering this maddening, ambiguous question by saying something like: 'The ultimate aim of a director of a permanent company is to create a situation where the collective intelligence and instinct of the group can eliminate the need to have a director at all; where ultimately, the actors, in tune with the author's material and the physical requirements of the production which express it, collectively assemble the artifact through a kind of unfailing aesthetic chemistry which is bred in their bone'. After a while, I stopped answering the question that way and eventually refused to answer it altogether. I came to believe that that was a kind of aesthetic hogwash, as my experience had demonstrated that the best theatrical results stemmed from some overall vision, the director's or the designer's, occasionally the author's, and that, although companies such as the Commedia dell' Arte or The Living Theatre could make a good case for illustrating the supremacy of a company intelligence, those kinds of results depended on a continuity and permanence, the luxury of which the contemporary theatre simply did not permit. Practically speaking, it was the ingenuity or inspiration of a director sensitive to the needs of his actors and his author that provided the plasticity with which a company could mould the best results.

But Peter's essay made me fiercely deconstruct that belief. If Brook, who epitomised the conceptual approach to theatre, could reach a pass where he eschewed 'personal expression' and came to rely upon some more free-wheeling approach which led to 'shared discovery', then perhaps my idealised image of a collective product and a directorless company was not as scatty as I originally thought. Maybe the intrinsic, primordial tendency of theatrical art *was* towards some rare balance between individual creativity and collective formulation. Maybe there *was* a way to express the multiplicity of meanings contained in a work of art without boiling them down into one single crucible. And maybe the brilliance of any single intepretation – whether an actor's or a director's – was merely the incandescence of a shooting star, whereas the real aim was to create the lustre of the entire firmament.

Because it was Brook who had posited this possibility and he had been such a formative influence, I hashed it over in my mind for a long time. Finally, I came to a conclusion, but even as I state it, I acknowledge the many hours of toing and froing which preceded it; and so, despite the clang of my conviction, I shall always, I suppose, be ready to return to the half-way house of painful reappraisals.

Brook's criticism about the partiality of individual interpretations is predicated on a groundless abstraction: namely that Shakespeare in some mystical sense equals and encompasses 'reality'. 'What he wrote,' says Brook, 'is not interpretation; it is the thing itself.' But this is merely a hyperbolic way of delivering a compliment to Shakespeare's variety and richness. Shakespeare's view of kingship, of religion, of honour, of heredity and of order represents a fairly typical set of Elizabethan opinions which are in no way peculiar to himself. In some instances, as in his questioning of divine infallibility, he may have been ahead of his time – but not uniquely so. There were many writers and artists who shared Shakespeare's view of the universe and his scepticism of its prevailing ideas. He was grounded in Renaissance sentiment and Renaissance thought, and many of his contemporaries fashioned viable and even brilliant plays from the same set of beliefs. Artistically speaking, there is no such thing as 'the thing itself'. Reality is comprehended by the artist and transmitted through acts of interpretation. The artist is not responsible for the tangible universe, only his perceptions of it. When these are well-founded and well-expressed, certain verities get enshrined in the writing – as was so often the case with Shakespeare. But Shakespeare did not create the Elizabethan notions of honour or heredity, of Christian mercy or salvation; he merely absorbed the ideas which were current in his time and turned them to good advantage. Without an understanding and opinion about Elizabethan society and its values (that is, reality) there would be no Shakespearian reality to convey, and that which is conveyed represents, like all works of art, merely the distillations and partial views of one person's experience. To claim as much as Brook claims for Shakespeare is to deify him. To claim that Shakespeare wrote 'the thing itself' is tantamount to saying that he is in some way more rooted in reality than

Jonson or Marlowe or Webster, whereas the fact is that he is merely rooted in his own reality – that which we aggrandise with the adjective 'Shakespearian' and which takes on particular connotations as soon as we compare his style of writing with those of his contemporaries.

Every production of a classic is a diminishment of the original, because every production of a play falls into given parameters: those laid down by a specific set of actors, a specific attitude on the part of the director and a specific predisposition on the part of the public. What is the opposite of a 'diminishment'? A play that realises the full potential of the work of art in every one of its many particulars! But, to achieve this, there has to be a comprehensiveness on the part of the artist which is simply inconceivable in human terms. Just as there can never be a definitive version of *Hamlet* because the passage of time and an audience's changing perceptions prevent the *definitive* from ever solidifying itself, so there can never be a production of a Shakespeare play which delivers all of its goods. Who is to say what all those goods consist of? With each generation, they change appreciably. In the nineteenth century, they consisted of scenic effects and sentimentality which, because these were rejected by succeeding generations, were no longer part of the bill of lading a hundred years later. Can one conceive of a production of Shakespeare which is simultaneously sumptious and spare, romantic and dark, pessimistic and optimistic, experimental and traditional? Although all of these qualities can, in some measure, be derived from the plays, they imply antithetical approaches which deliver contrasting results. Although the plays are capable of assimilating a variety of different approaches, they cannot do so *all at once*, despite the fact that all these qualities lie nestled in the works as potentialities. Every production is partial and different: that is the glory of Shakespeare, that there is no end to the permutations. But that is quite different from asking for a kind of Omnibus Shakespeare in which every conceivable Shakespearian seed has sprouted and is in full bloom. Variety and contradiction is all we know of Shakespeare, and all we need to know.

If the single vision of the director is to be scrapped in favour of 'shared discovery', what is the mechanism by which this discovery is to be activated? Brook says that 'a production of Shakespeare could go far beyond the unity that one man's imagination could give'. Then why have the 'one man' there in the first place? If a collective intelligence uninfluenced by the 'likes or dislikes' of a director can bring about this 'shared discovery', surely the presence of that 'one man' is not only redundant but an obstacle to the group will. The logical conclusion of Brook's argument is a production without the fertilising agent of one man's conception. But Brook has not removed himself from the process; he has (according to his own argument) merely subordinated himself to the group will – the same will, it must be stated, that he created and conditioned through months of actor training and aesthetic insinuation. The alternative to the director merely showing his own image of the play, says Brook, is not handing over the entire process to the collective but giving it over to 'another process' – unnamed – 'which starts always with the instinctive feeling the play needs to be done now.'

The implication appears to be that the immediacy or topicality of the play – its need 'to be done now' – will in some way provide the creative substitute to the single-minded director bent on his personal interpretation. But *The Mahabharata* was conceived by Brook and, over a period of about a decade, realised by a company and a playwright working through his comprehension of the project. There was no apparent 'immediacy' or sense of it having 'to be done now' and, if there was, it was sustained for almost a decade. In his work on *The Cherry Orchard*, the director working with a variety of sociological and historical materials and in concert with a great number of collaborators, tried to discover the 'myth' or 'secret play' which nestled within conventional perceptions of Chekhov's work. But the fruits of all these researches were distilled to actors in the usual way – through trial and error proceeding from a creative preconception; that is, to scrape away the Chekhovian overlay of some hundred years in order to discover the true play beneath. This is a conventional working premise in the theatre, although not everyone achieves the kind of distinction Brook brought to his production. And no matter what personal contributions may have been made by actors during the process, their refinement and distillation remained the work of the director, even if, as was probably the case, the actor was unaware that he was excavating in a mineshaft originally sunk by another.

As much as one would like to believe that there is a dynamic alternative to 'personal expression' and 'one man's interpretation', I do not see – nor has Brook provided – the blueprints for this alternative *modus operandi*. That it can exist, and *should* exist, I would not quarrel with for a moment.

Wrestling

10 with Jan Kott

··

The beefy brunette, her skin glistening with Krisko cooking-oil, held the brawny blonde in an impregnable hammerlock. After a couple of perfunctory twists, the blonde was supine and the brunette, now astride her stomach, began pulling out her hair. The crowd, mostly raucous college boys and beer-swilling regulars, cheered and whistled as the triumphant brunette, imitating the action of a piston, pounced heavily on the blonde's abdomen. In a moment, two other female contenders drenched in mud would begin the main event of the evening.

At a ringside table in the Hollywood Tropicana Club, the sleazy mecca of female mud wrestling in Los Angeles, I sat with Professor Jan Kott, recent recipient of the George Jean Nathan Award for drama criticism and, arguably, one of the finest Shakespearian scholars of his day. Kott, an old friend from London, having declined all invitations to theatres and concerts, had asked me to arrange tickets for the mud wrestling and he was clearly mesmerised by the ritual of men paying for the privilege of massaging female combatants before they laid into each other in the makeshift ring.

When we left the club, he coolly elucidated the qualities of the evening, clearly impressed by the order of the highly-structured social situation: men sheepishly keeping their hands at their sides while bikini-clad Amazons, in return for cash, planted hot, sweaty kisses onto their lips, and muscular bodyguards stood by to make sure erotic stimuli never gave way to tactile contact.

'It's very much like Elizabethan bear-baiting,' said Kott. 'An atmosphere of abandon and sexual aggression but firmly suppressed and performed strictly according to the rules.'

If one knew Jan Kott, it would be no surprise that of all the entertainments offered in Los Angeles, he would choose the raunchy art of Female Mud Wrestling. In Scotland, when I first met him, he claimed to have found the origins of medieval tavern theatre in an Edinburgh pub. Kott, the Shakespearian critic with the greatest influence on the stage, has been a controversial and wilfully off-beat scholar since he first came to prominence in 1964, with his book *Shakespeare, Our Contemporary*. Directors such as Peter Brook, Ariane Mnouchkine and Georgio Strehler openly acknowledge their debt to him and his most recent books, *The Theatre of Essence* and *The Bottom Translation*, refortified the reputation first established over two decades ago.

The following is an edited transcript of a dialogue we had in his apartment in Santa Monica while he was in California as a visiting Getty Scholar. Professor Kott speaks what is best described as non-syntactical, Slavic-styled broken English and, to a certain extent, I was obliged to 'translate' his words into their English equivalent. However, for the sake of accuracy, I have asked him to survey the gist of his answers and the following represents my perception of his replies, verified by his own corrections and emendations.

MAROWITZ

Are there particular plays of Shakespeare which, for one reason or another, become relevant at particular times in history and, if so, which ones are particularly relevant today?

KOTT

To my mind, all of Shakespeare's plays – or almost all – are relevant, but, at certain times, some works become more contemporary than others. Take *Hamlet*, for instance, a play which has been popular for many generations but which, in the Romantic period, took on an increased popularity in Europe. The other striking example would be *Troilus and Cressida*; a play which had been performed very rarely in England up until the start of the Second World War. During the Munich period, when Chamberlain signed the non-aggression pact with Hitler, *Troilus and Cressida* became, for the young people and for the intelligentsia, a very contemporary work. From my own experience in Poland, the most contemporary Shakespearian plays have been *Richard II* and *Richard III* – because they deal with what's been called 'the great mechanism', terror, dictatorship, etc. and one tended to identify events in the play with Stalin's purges, the great massacres, despots who claw their way to the top and then quickly topple into the abyss.

MAROWITZ

Is there a Shakespearian work today which is, as it were, *becoming* contemporary because of its affinities with current events?

KOTT

In the past decade, there are at least two Shakespearian plays that have sort of made new careers for themselves. One was *Titus Andronicus* and the other, even more so, *Timon of Athens* – plays which, rarely performed before, have taken on a new kind of relevance for modern audiences. *The Winter's Tale* must also be included; a play even less frequently performed which has, in the past ten years or so, begun to carry a new message and a new fascination; probably because of a new temporal attitude which has developed in regard to Shakespeare. There is some obscurity or darkness in this play which has now become dazzling and tempting. This is also true of *The Tempest*, but for different reasons.

MAROWITZ

And what are those?

KOTT

One has to do with technological advances in the theatre itself. If one approaches this play traditionally, seeing Prospero as a kind of old magus or enchanted Santa Claus figure, it's of course ridiculous. If we try to make this island merely a kind of enchanted Disneyland, it's just childish. But with the new technology, with lasers and video and other 'special effects', *The Tempest* becomes ripe for a whole range of new theatrical possibilities. But there is also a new *thematic* incentive in regard to this play which lends itself to a different ideological interpretation; a new definition of magic, of art, of the power of art, the secrecy of art, the obscurity of art, the creation and re-creation of art, of Theatre as art, and, symbolically, of Creation itself.

MAROWITZ

Is it possible for Shakespeare's works to be constantly reinterpreted or does there come a saturation-point; a point at which one simply has to return to the traditional understanding of these plays?

KOTT

I don't believe in the idea of some staple tradition in Shake-speare, either theatrical or interpretive, which cannot be changed or challenged. First of all, the Shakespearian tradition does not exist. It was lost because of the rupture brought about by the closing of the theatres during Cromwell's time.

MAROWITZ

Does that mean then there's no such thing as a traditional rendering of a Shakesperian play?

KOTT

If one believed there could be some kind of traditional interpreta-tion of Shakespeare, it would have to be in English, but now we have a theatre of the planet – with festivals and revivals in every conceivable part of the world. Shakespeare exists now in Africa, in India, in Japan – almost any country you care to name.

MAROWITZ

Do you mean that because Shakespeare has become multinational-ised – mixed up with so many different cultures and theatrical styles – that it is impossible any longer to conceive of a traditional approach?

KOTT

Yes.

MAROWITZ

But isn't it possible through translation to essay a traditional view of Shakespeare's plays? That's to say, a rendition of what we take to be the historically-based, received perception of those works?

KOTT

No, I don't believe so, and the reason is similar to that which applies to ancient Greek tragedy. We no longer have the tools that were available to a theatre such as the Globe: the wooden 'O', the sexual disguise of boys playing woman's parts, etc. just as we no longer have the amphitheatres which created, and to a certain extent conditioned, the Greek drama. We now have a new medium. The old medium, if merely repeated, creates only museum art.

MAROWITZ

So, by freeing these plays from their original conventions, we have, in a sense *made* them universal, is that what you mean?

KOTT

Yes, I mean just that.

MAROWITZ

Is it necessary for directors mounting Shakespeare to take account of the plays' historicity? Or is it possible for a director to proceed with no regard whatsoever to the given historical and political background of the works?

KOTT

There are no rules. It's really a free-for-all. It has a lot to do with the *number* of Shakespearian productions. If you have only one production of *Hamlet* a year then, for the sake of the schools, the colleges, the new audience, it has to be what you might call a 'regular' *Hamlet*. But when you have twenty in a year, even if it were possible to produce a 'traditional' *Hamlet*, there would be no point in producing twenty identical *Hamlets*.

MAROWITZ

But I mean something else. Let's say a director is preparing a production of *Hamlet*; is it really possible for him to ignore the Elizabethan attitudes towards kingship, towards inheritance, towards honour and chivalry – in short, towards all the fundamental values that pertained at that time, and still do justice to the original work?

KOTT

I don't know. It seems to me this is different in regard to different Shakespearian plays. It's not the same in the case of the histories, for instance, or in a play such as *Macbeth*, where you have a king, a royal family, feudal lords, a tower, the landscape of Scotland; elements which exist in the matter of the play. If you transpose all of this into a Sheikdom, let's say, or into some other highly exotic cultural clime, much of the play will become vague or insubstantial. On the other hand, if you take a play like *The Comedy of Errors*, and obediently respect the historical milieu of the work, it will be impossible or boring or, at the very least, irrelevant. We have to place this play into some kind of new environment.

MAROWITZ

So there are plays of Shakespeare that are pliant and others in which one cannot so easily break the closed circuit of the original work?

KOTT

This is exactly my meaning. In the historical plays, the essence of history should be respected – but the essence of feudal history is not necessarily the sad tales of the Lord's Anointed. It is dishonest to perform *Richard III* or *Richard II* or *Henry IV* without touching on certain parallels to our contemporary time of political terrors, 'les temps des assassins' etc.

MAROWITZ

So even if one tried to present a traditional–historical version of *Richard III*, contemporary associations in the minds of the audience would still be informing the play. People coming to see *Richard III* would still come with the knowledge of Stalin and East Europe and Afghanistan.

KOTT

You see, the conscious director has to ask himself: what is the historicity, and what the contemporaneity of the play? In *Richard III*, for example, what is *contemporary* is the terror and the persecution; the experience of fear, danger, torture, the entire mechanism of political repression. But the icons of this terror are, of course, the old kings of England. It would be risky to make the face of *Richard III* identical with the face of Josef Stalin. But it would be blind and childish to say this is merely the remote past of the feudal era. Sometimes the analogy is stronger if the identification is not too obvious. Mnouchkine in her last productions of Shakespeare's histories dressed the English kings and Court as samurai in the costumes of the Kabuki. This oriental masquerade seems to me pretentious. It's not the costumes that are so important or the 'faces' of the Lord's Anointed, but the mechanism of terror. *Its* faces are both historical and timeless.

MAROWITZ

So historicity and contemporaneity must go hand in hand in every legitimate classical revival?

KOTT

Exactly.

MAROWITZ

Then tell me this. What is scholarship's role in relation to Shakespearian production? Should the scholar be a kind of hovering dramaturge, as for instance you were in regard to the National Theatre production of *As You Like It* and Peter Brook's *King Lear*? What kind of function can he or should he perform?

KOTT

Again, there are no rules. The ideal dramaturge would combine the skills of both the director and the scholar. But either such people do not exist or cannot exist, or, in any case, are very hard to find.

MAROWITZ

I'm very aware of a sharp division between professional theatrical production and scholarship. When I occasionally attend symposia or academic get-togethers, I always feel I'm with people from a different solar system than myself. Does such a division have to exist?

KOTT

There are a few outstanding exceptions to the rule: Granville-Barker, for instance, who wrote intelligently and even academically on the subject of Shakespeare and was, by all accounts, an excellent director. There's also John Russell Brown, who is an excellent scholar and also a professional director. Then there's Georgio Strehler, whose knowledge of the Italian and Renaissance theatre is utterly limitless, and who is also one of the great theatre directors. But I take your point, it's hard to come up with too many examples. It's rather hard to find someone who is a virgin and also very good in bed.

MAROWITZ

This role of the 'dramaturge' is a very imprecise one. More and more, people feel there should be such a creature attached to a serious theatre, but no one is too sure of precisely how he should function there. How do you see his role?

KOTT

Again, there are no rules. A dramaturge is a German invention, which probably began in the nineteenth century when Goethe was appointed to the Court Theatre at Weimar. There are many possible kinds of working relationships. It's up to the director to hammer out a viable relationship with his dramaturge – one that will work for both of them. But the director, you have to remember, is concerned with acting on stage, bodies in movement. Footnotes exist in a scholastic work; but it's impossible to have them in the theatre. A director can't say: I'm doing it this way, but I could just as easily do it this other way. The director has to choose his line and then hoe to it. The director, of course, is second only to God – and, in some instances, even before Him, so to work out a good relationship with a dramaturge is very difficult. It's more difficult even than marriage – and marriage, as we all know, is difficult enough.

MAROWITZ

In a lot of recent Shakespeare productions, there has been a new emphasis on decor. It's almost as if stage-setting, in the nineteenth-century sense, has returned to our stage. Does this have some kind of special implication?

KOTT

Two or three years ago, during a Shakespeare Festival at Stratford, Ontario, I saw an extremely elaborate production of *A Midsummer Night's Dream* – very rich settings – in many ways reminiscent of Max Reinhardt's production of the thirties. With the rotation of taste, after years of naked sets and spartan decor, the effect of this sumptious and elaborate setting was to give us something new and interesting. That's the first point. The second is: in the last decade, there has been an enormous advance in opera – I mean opera as spectacle. When I was young, opera seemed very old-fashioned, very nineteenth-century, something that you went to hear rather than to see. Today it's become highly advanced, extremely elaborate and dominantly visual. Whereas before, the opera was in many ways aping the theatre, now the theatre seems to be aping opera. And, of course, many theatre directors such as Zeffirelli, Peter Hall, Peter Brook to a certain extent, move easily from one to the other. In my lifetime, that's to say since about the end of World War II, there was an ideological and philosophical emphasis on contemporary inter-pretation in Shakespeare; an emphasis on thematic content, on what these plays mean and *should* mean to modern audiences. And now, because of a certain distrust or disenchantment with ideology, a certain boredom with politics, there is this return to a Shakespeare which is apolitical, non-philosophic, non-ideological. And since the plays no longer have 'new meanings', they must at least have new costumes, new settings, new visual expression.

MAROWITZ

So you believe this new emphasis on decor is a compensation for lack of thematic substance?

KOTT

By and large, I would say so. If not a new message, then at least there should be some new tricks. Remember in *The Tempest*, when Ariel says to Prospero: 'what would my potent master? Here I am.' and Prospero replies: 'Thou and thy meaner fellows your last service/Did worthily perform, and I must use you/in such another trick. Go bring the rabble . . .'

MAROWITZ

But is it a general rule that, when you have an extremely elaborate setting, it is concealing a paucity of real content? Aren't there certain kinds of interpretations that demand more elaborate settings – merely to fulfil certain ambitious visual intentions?

KOTT

Probably you are right – but there's another point here. It's not only that this tendency indicates the end of ideological interpretations; it also marks, in some way, the end of the old avant-garde; by that I mean the avant-garde of the fifties and the sixties. The proponents of this avant-garde were, more or less, restricted to small theatres, the limited resources of the small stage; they weren't involved with large spectacles. Now, with the termination of this avant-garde, we are seeing a return to the big spectacle, Robert Wilson being perhaps the most obvious example of the new avant-garde – an artist whose work demands an extremely expensive, extremely spectacular theatrical form.

MAROWITZ

It is certainly the impression today that someone like Robert Wilson is the most conspicuous exponent of the 'new' avant-garde, but is his work, strictly speaking, avant-garde? Is it not an amalgam of influences derived from the sixties and seventies and even earlier? Does his work represent a genuine move in another direction or is it merely a grandiloquent recapitulation of the 'happenings' and multi-media experiments of twenty and twenty-five years ago?

KOTT

No comment.

MAROWITZ

I'd like, despite your reticence, to push this subject a little further. I agree with you that today there is nothing quite so clapped-out as the 'avant-garde' work of the sixties. My question is: can any avant-garde replenish itself quite so quickly? Don't a certain number of generations have to go by, assimilating the innovations, before the next wave of the avant-garde can appear?

Is it actually possible for each generation, every ten years or so, to produce its own avant-garde?

KOTT
It's very hard to answer this because the avant-garde is not simply a new batch of tricks thrown up by the new generation, but a challenge thrown down to the morality, the philosophy, the manners, and the *status quo*. It is difficult to imagine an avant-garde without a challenge to established values, or, indeed, to the Establishment itself.

MAROWITZ
Do you see this happening today?

KOTT
I personally do not see it.

MAROWITZ
Would you agree then that, in a sense, the old avant-garde of the fifties and sixties has not, in fact, produced any discernible successors?

KOTT
I can only say that, speaking for myself, I cannot see any significant avant-garde movement in the original sense of that over-used term. But I must admit that, for the past five or six years, I have been very cut off from the mainstream.

MAROWITZ
Is this perhaps because it is no longer possible to challenge established values, to 'épater le bourgeois' as used to be done in the last fifty to a hundred years?

KOTT
But who is the 'bourgeois' today? It is the avant-garde itself.

MAROWITZ
Is it conceivable that the kinds of insurrections we associate with the old avant-garde, which were so culturally disturbing and artistically revolutionary, are no longer possible in a day and age where society is inured to all such shocks?

KOTT
Probably yes, because, as we have all seen in the past decade or so, the bourgeois market-place is all-powerful; it consumes the avant-garde, as it consumes everything else. There is no

innovation, no new invention that isn't, in a matter of weeks, packaged, merchandised and distributed to the mainstream society.

MAROWITZ

Is it then the genius of that highly-commercialised society to be able to gobble up avant-garde initiative so rapidly that no challenge to established values can threaten it for very long?

KOTT

I guess so. There was an article in *The New York Times* several months ago about some marvellous new painting which was considered a remarkable specimen of avant-garde work, and it was immediately on sale, the very next week. What can one say about that when one considers the fate of early avant-garde paintings that had to wait decades for sale, and almost a hundred years for recognition?

MAROWITZH

I want to return to the subject of Shakespeare. I know that Brook's *King Lear* was very much influenced by your book *Shakespeare, Our Contemporary*, as was Georgio Strehler's *Tempest* and the National Theatre's production of *As You Like It*. Isn't there something suspect and a bit second-hand about a director basing a production on another man's ideas? Doesn't this in some vague way smack of plagiarism?

KOTT

No, not to my mind. Because, as we all know, a theatrical production, from no matter how innovative a director, looks for its nourishment wherever it can find it – in current events, in politics, in personal experience, theatrical experience, and so on. Peter Brook, who is a genius of eclecticism, is perhaps the best example of this.

MAROWITZ

So you think that taking ideas from a work of scholarship is just part and parcel of the overall plagiarism a director indulges in when he assembles a production in the first place?

KOTT

Yes, because the very essence of the director's work is plagiarism. He plagiarises the text; he plagiarises the theatrical tradition; he plagiarises the experience of his actors. He almost cannot make a move without plagiarising something or somebody. A theatrical production is, almost by definition, a second-hand work of art.

MAROWITZ

Would you therefore deduce from that, that a director can never be an original creator, but can only be, at best, something of an inspired eclectic?

KOTT

Some directors create their own theatre. Some of them not only devise *mise-en-scène*, but create their own physical environment as well, and the theatrical styles that are performed there. So much so that the next generation spends most of its time plagiarising *their* work. Take Meyerhold, for example. Many of the directors who came after him were the legitimate or illegitimate children of Meyerhold. Stanislavsky has thousands of legitimate and illegitimate children – especially in this country. Grotowski has certainly had his plagiarisers. Take Brecht – who, to my mind, was the man most responsible for changing the attitudes to Shakespeare in England. It was the Brechtian vision and to a certain extent the Brechtian technology which heavily influenced the staging of Shakespeare all over Europe – from Poland to England.

MAROWITZ

But what of Brecht's dialectical approach to material – what made him so uniquely Brechtian – do you see that influence as well? Because otherwise, it's just a superficial influence you're referring to.

KOTT

I don't believe it's all that superficial; not when one is dealing with a new style of acting, a new way of using the stage. The old message and the old vision – meaning, function and spectacle – were challenged. If you try to deal with Shakespearian drama, not through an understanding of the characters but rather through the objective situation which asks us to see the 'unnatural of the natural' as Brecht used to say, that doesn't produce a superficial impact.

MAROWITZ

Can you cite productions under Brecht's influence which have reconstituted the material in that way; have made us see it more objectively and from that different perspective?

KOTT

Yes, in many of the British and Italian productions we often get a Brechtian vision, though never the Brechtian ideology.

MAROWITZ

To return then to my earlier point: do you think it is legitimate to be Brechtian in appearance and not Brechtian in ideology?

KOTT

Even during Brecht's own term at the Berliner Ensemble, there were productions which have been true to the Brechtian form but extremely alien to Brecht's ideology. The best example of this is *Mother Courage*, which never quite achieved the contempt Brecht wanted in regard to his central character.

MAROWITZ

Are you saying that Brecht himself was never able to produce a truly Brechtian result in his work?

KOTT

In some ways, yes. The question is still open. But the main heritage of Brecht in the modern theatre is not the political pretensions of Brecht's work, the assault on capitalism etc., but the theatrical matter, the Epic approach that relied heavily on the 'alienation effect' which is perhaps the most important part of the acting legacy.

MAROWITZ

I want to ask you about certain tendencies in classical interpretations. Can Kurosawa's *Ran* really be considered a version of *King Lear*, given the fact that it veers away so radically from the original work? At what point does an extrapolation of a Shakespearian work, such as Edward Bond's *Lear* or Tom Stoppard's *Rosencrantz and Guildenstern are Dead* or Grotowski's *Doctor Faustus* become an independent work of art with no debt at all to the original?

KOTT

Lévi-Strauss once said: 'Every interpretation of a myth is a new myth.' For example, the Freudian version of the Oedipus and Elektra myths is a new version of those myths in this larger sense, any *Antigone* (and we've had about twenty Antigones in modern times) or any *Elektra* (and there have been several of those in recent years) is a reinterpretation, or rethinking of the original Greek play.

MAROWITZ

But that is an extrapolation from a myth. What we were talking about is an extrapolation from a given literary work by William Shakespeare.

KOTT

The only real difference between Shakespeare and the Greek tragedians is that Shakespeare is somewhat closer to us in time. In any case, to my way of thinking, we have to challenge Shakespeare – even if not actually challenging the words themselves. The interpretation should give new meaning without changing the letter of the text. Once I wrote; 'We need to rape classics without respect but with love and passion.' Now, I would qualify that by saying: we have to force the classical texts to give us new answers. But to obtain new answers, we have to bombard them with new questions. If Shakespeare is translated into Japanese or Hebrew, obviously the director's freedom is greater. If we change the medium from stage to screen, for instance, our freedom is greater still because it is impossible, or just silly, merely to transplant a stage production onto the screen.

MAROWITZ

But to return to Kurosawa . . .

KOTT

To my mind, the greatest, most impressive and illuminating vision of *Macbeth* is Kurosawa's *Throne of Blood*.

MAROWITZ

And you would still contend that, even though it radically veers away from the original, it is still, in essence, Shakespeare's play?

KOTT

Kurosawa's film *Ran* is much further away from the play than Peter Brook's film version of *King Lear*. In some ways, Kurosawa is more faithful to Shakespeare in his movie than Peter Brook is in his. This is also true of Kozintzev's *King Lear*, which is, to my mind, one of the greatest screen adaptations of all time.

MAROWITZ

What pops into my mind is a film of the late forties with, I believe, Paul Douglas, called *Joe Macbeth*, which was a gangster movie which bore almost no relation to Shakespeare's play but dealt with the rise of a small-time gangster who rubbed out all the other gangsters who stood in his way in order to become top dog. Would you say that a film like that is also a legitimate extrapolation from *Macbeth*?

KOTT

No.

MAROWITZ

Then what is the dividing-line between an original, independent work and a valid interpretation of a Shakespearian play?

KOTT

I can answer that best by posing another question: Is *West Side Story* a legitimate interpretation of *Romeo and Juliet* or a completely new work?

MAROWITZ

The answer for me would be that it's a completely new work.

KOTT

I don't know what a 'completely new work' is. Shakespeare is always there in the background. One cannot completely obliterate him.

MAROWITZ

It would appear then, from what you're saying, that one has to examine each one of these 'extrapolations' or 'versions' on its own merits. *The Comedy of Errors* is not *The Boys From Syracuse*, but this musical has taken Shakespeare's comedy as its springboard, just as, I suppose, Shakespeare took Plautus as *his* springboard. So does one say to Shakespeare: 'Thank you very much for providing us with this story, but we don't really need you any longer as we're going off in another direction?' In just the same way as Shakespeare might have said 'thank you' to Belleforest or Kyd or Holinshed or Boccaccio?

KOTT

Exactly.

MAROWITZ

Let me ask you this. Do you think that being a Polish critic with a European background gives you a different kind of insight into Shakespeare's work? You have Polish eyes. Does that make you see something different than if you had British or American eyes?

KOTT

I would suppose at least fifty per cent of what I've written was because of my Polish and European experience. First of all, there's the social and political context of my life. I was in Warsaw with the underground during World War Two and was constantly involved in politics during the time I lived in Poland. And so, naturally, I am a completely different bird compared to the British or American critics. Half of my life experience has been politics rather than books or spectacles; immersion in real history, not history seen in film or television documentaries.

MAROWITZ

Can you take that one step further and say why it is that you see different things in Shakespeare's works?

KOTT

I guess the best answer to that is to quote what Peter Brook wrote in his introduction to my first book. He said: 'Kott is undoubtedly the only writer on Elizabethan matters who assumes without question that every one of his readers will at some point or other have been woken by the police in the middle of the night.'

MAROWITZ

But can that also mean, given your natural and instinctive political bias, you sometimes see things in Shakespeare's works which are not there?

KOTT

All partial views are, at the same time, important and incorrect.

MAROWITZ

And if one wanted to provide a corrective?

KOTT

It's virtually impossible for a director, and even more so for a critic, to be 'correct'. If someone wants to be 'correct', they must become a proof-reader and not a critic.

MAROWITZ

Do you mean then there is no such thing as 'correct' criticism?

KOTT

To the best of my knowledge, no such thing exists. Real criticism cannot be, what you would call, correct.

MAROWITZ

Is there such a thing as fallacious criticism?

KOTT

No. If one is not correct, it doesn't follow that one is fallacious. In my mind, not to be 'correct' means a critic may defend, in a more vigorous way than is usually done by so-called impartial critics, the views that he holds. As a critic, you have to be a partisan. In some way, a critic is an advocate or an attorney, but never the presiding judge. He has either to accuse or to defend. No one expects the attorney to be completely fair, because his function is either to accuse or to defend. The virtue of fairness is not one of the virtues of the critic.

MAROWITZ

To take up your own metaphor: there comes a point at the end of a trial when what attornies have defended or prosecuted becomes the subject of a judgement. Is there some final tribunal for critical ideas where they are ultimately judged to be right or wrong? Correct or incorrect?

KOTT

This just does not exist.

MAROWITZ

The prosecution and the defence *do* exist, but the judgement does not?

KOTT

There are no final judgements in criticism.

MAROWITZ

What, fundamentally, is the use of Shakespeare criticism?

KOTT

The most obvious answer, which was once formulated by T. B. Spencer at a Royal Shakespeare conference, is: Shakespeare has three lives. His first life is the theatre. His second life consists of his written works, published and read from one generation to the next, and his third life consists of teaching and criticism. For millions of students all over the world, Shakespeare exists as a text and as a subject for study. It may be sensible or nonsensical, intelligible or unintelligible, but what one cannot deny is that Shakespeare exists, he is a living presence. The average young man who is exposed to Shakespeare during his school or college years, and eventually becomes an old man, keeps some portion of Shakespeare with him to the end of his life.

MAROWITZ

But what use is he to this young and subsequently old man? Is Shakespeare *philosophically* important to him? Is his humanism of some value? What is it that's so important about this heritage?

KOTT

Trivially speaking, Shakespeare is a supermarket. Shakespeare criticism produces Shakespeare scholars; Shakespeare scholars produce Shakespeare criticism, which in turn produces Shakespeare teachers who go on to become Shakespeare critics and Shakespeare scholars, and so forth and so on in endless repetition.

MAROWITZ

It's one of the great multi-national industries.

KOTT

Of course. Shakespeare was presumably born in Stratford, but if someone should prove that he wasn't born in Stratford or that there never was such a person, it would be a disaster – not only culturally, but financially as well.

MAROWITZ

If Shakespeare, it should turn out, were born in Liverpool, let's say, it would be . . .

KOTT

An international catastrophe!

MAROWITZ

You seem to be saying that Shakespeare is like a self-perpetuating and unkillable Frankenstein monster.

KOTT

In some ways, yes. But that is equally true of the universities. As I wrote once, they live by 'eating': eating Aristotle, eating Plato, eating Molière, eating Shakespeare. It's a gargantuan digestive system.

MAROWITZ

And they also disgorge at regular intervals.

KOTT

Without Shakespeare, it would mean the downfall of one-third of the American educational system. He is in many ways the most established figure in the Establishment.

MAROWITZ

Will Shakespeare always be our contemporary, or is it conceivable to you that a time might come when Shakespeare will no longer speak to modern generations? Could Shakespeare become like Seneca or Terence or Menander – someone archaic, whose influence might just pass away?

KOTT

My dear Charles, I will have been many, many years dead before anything like that comes to pass.

Seven American
11 m*is*conceptions

· ·

1. Shakespearian production is no different from any other kind of theatre

One of the most deep-rooted instincts in America is the need to debunk what it cannot comprehend. In regard to the classics, the American suspicion of 'high art' takes the form of levelling down anything that appears to be lofty or high-falutin'. This accounts for the widespread notion that a Shakespearian play is really no different from any other, and there is no reason in the world why a knotty and intractable work such as *King Lear* or *The Tempest* should not be approached as if it were an item from the *œuvre* of Kaufman and Hart, Arthur Miller or even Neil Simon. As a result, all questions of prosody – scansion, metre, pulse etc. – are given short shrift. The American actor understands prose (that's where it all runs together, right?) and he has a working definition of blank verse which, loosely stated is: ta dum, ta dum, ta dum, ta dum, ta dum – five beats to a line – the stress on the second beat. Iambic pentameter – what could be easier?

By refusing to acknowledge that the rules of prosody are more complex than his abbreviated understanding of them, the American actor (and director) swan blithely into the most treacherous waters and usually sink without trace. Even if they mastered the structure of Shakespearian poetry, there are other, less tangible factors in the plays which are as far removed from psychological realism as Des Moines is from Stratford-upon-Avon. Size, for instance, which in practical terms means that characters in classical works, distanced by time and embroiled in epic actions, cannot be reduced to the room-size dimensions encouraged by American theatre training and espoused by The Method; that a Hamlet, a Macbeth, a Lear or a Falstaff cannot simply be wedged into a three-dimensional, naturalistically-observed acting container on the assumption that modern parallels will automatically produce classical equivalents. More pertinent still: that in the revival of any Shakespearian work, contemporary practitioners have to match up historicity with contemporaneity, so that the present does not shortchange the past. It is the notion that Shakespeare is merely the realistic drama writ large that produces the travesties, distortions and diminutions which subvert classical work in most American theatres.

2. Shakespeare is entirely different from any other kind of theatre

Behind every work of art, if it communicates itself, there must be certain patterns of behaviour, feelings and motives with which an audience can identify. A classic has these in spades – and that is why the plays have lasted as long as they have. Each succeeding generation has been able to recognise moods, emotions and relationships they know intimately from their own lives and times. If they did not, these plays would not survive, as indeed many plays from the same period, which do not achieve such identifications, do not. So clearly, there is a recognisable realistic foundation on which all durable classics rest.

However the similarities are less relevant than the differences, for Shakespearian works have a multiplicity of meanings and a variety of styles which put them in a different category from the more attenuated, two-dimensional works of the modern theatre. Let us take the obvious differences first.

Many of the characters are regal or legendary, epic or outsize. Their circumstances are in many ways more charged and more remote than characters we encounter in the plays of Miller, Williams, Mamet or Simon. The events which develop these characters are heftier than those that motivate modern characters who want to marry well, resolve a personal conflict or overcome a social pressure. Because many of Shakespeare's characters 'represent' larger issues – like kingship or honour – their dilemmas are played out on a larger canvas where more is at stake. To embody that *more*, actors and directors have to achieve a greater breadth of characterisation. Their turmoils have to match up to the language and circumstances which embody them.

In Shakespearian works, you also have the phenomenon, peculiar to Elizabethan dramatists, of switching rapidly between the rhetorical and the lyrical, the domestic and the regal, the private and the public, the poetic and the mundane. These shifts are what make Shakespeare's works so rich, and the inability to ring these changes is what impoverishes their theatrical expression. So, although no theatre can be extra-galactic – in the sense that it does not reflect people, situations and concerns comprehensible to its audience – there is a plateau which has to be reached before the works of Shakespeare can deliver the full weight of their artistic baggage. In that sense, Shakespearian production is just like every other kind of theatre and, at the same time, very different.

3. Only the British can properly perform the works of Shakespeare

The American paranoia in regard to Shakespeare dates back to the nineteenth century, when actors such as Booth and Forrest, touring in England, were outgunned and out-manoeuvred by artists such as Kean and Macready. And yet it was Edwin Booth who actually ushered in the more realistic style which was eventually exported to England and influenced Irving, Forbes-Robertson and, ultimately Gielgud, Richardson, Scofield and Olivier. The tempering of the bombastic force which used to pervade British acting is due, in large measure, to the nineteenth-century American influence – just as The Method's insistence on felt emotionalism influenced and is influencing contemporary classical acting.

There is no question that the techniques honed by the Royal Shakespeare Company over a period of twenty years, and ultimately adopted by the National Theatre and other British classical companies, constitute the finest balance between solid technique and powerhouse feeling. The British have the great advantage not only of 'speaking the language' but of instinctively understanding its cultural nuances. What, in the Victorian age, they lost and never quite recovered, is the gusto and passion which informed the Elizabethan and Jacobean periods and is no longer a prominent feature of the British character. The Americans have never lost it. It is a staple of the national character. And although the people in Shakespeare's plays still speak like Britons, they 'feel' and 'act' like Americans – that is to say, obsessively, athletically, dramatically and emotionally.

For these reasons, the American actor is temperamentally better suited to the works of William Shakespeare than is his

British counterpart. When he fails to achieve results, it is because he has not taken the time and trouble to master the technical requirements of the text or reach the scale on which the works have been conceived. At such time as the American actor begins to comprehend and master the structure of the Shakespearian canon, there will be no stopping him. He already has the physical and emotional equipment for great classical acting, but his lack of intelligence is contemptible, and, without intellect, there is no way of realising what is best in Shakespeare.

4. The only way to approach Shakespeare is to contemporise him

The single greatest American failing in regard to Shakespeare production is the idea that, in order to make Shakespeare more palatable to American audiences, graphic and convenient parallels have to be found. The American genius for innovation and experiment hits its nadir in the weird and grotesque permutations American directors foist onto the plays in their misguided attempts to popularise them. In most cases, these are external 'period' changes – the old works gussied up in the most unexpected attire and set in the most startling 'new' settings. It is because the American actor cannot play Shakespeare 'straight' that his innovations are so pathetic. For without coming to grips with the requirements of the language – which subsumes, of course, the necessities of characterisation – you cannot begin to slant or re-angle the original works. You *can* of course, but it looks like what it is: an attempt to circumvent the problems of the plays by diverting attention to their superficies. If, in the midst of the wildest and wackiest classical reinterpretations, the verse carried and the themes were preserved, that would go a long way towards validating the 'ground-breaking' reinterpretations; but when they do not, it is like a tone-deaf musician without the skills of melody or harmony essaying his own version of a standard.

A Shakespearian play poses a powerful challenge to a contemporary interpreter. A way of avoiding that challenge is to duck the play's central issues through novelty and innovation. A way of accepting it is by rethinking the material in contemporary terms and then expressing the seventeenth-century perception through a twentieth-century sensibility; but to do that, of course, American directors must first possess *perception* and *sensibility*, whereas, in most cases, these qualities are usurped by ostentation and oversimplification.

5. The only correct way to stage Shakespeare is to adopt the traditional approach

In 1642, the theatres of London were closed by the Puritans and they remained closed for some twenty years. When they re-opened, the 'tradition' which had begun with the reign of Queen Elizabeth and the establishment of The Lord Chamberlain's and Lord Admiral's Companies was effectively broken. The Restoration did not restore the Shakespearian tradition which flourished at The Theatre, The Curtain and The Globe, but created a new one conditioned by a different temperament, one which was the first to 'take liberties' with the plays of the past. It is significant to remember that, from the very first moment Shakespeare was being revived, he was being rethought and reinterpreted.

Strictly speaking, there *is* no tradition to maintain; none that contemporary actors and directors can discern. There is only the conservative view of the works, as opposed to the liberal. The first urges something called 'fidelity to the text' – which is a contradiction as the only way to interpret any text is to mingle it with the sensibilities and temperaments of the men and women trying to express it. As soon as one does this, the question of 'fidelity' vanishes in a flux of subjective interpretation. The liberals may be too free-wheeling for some people's taste, but it is only a matter of degree, for there is no way of staging the works of Shakespeare without grinding them through the mincers of artists' imagination. Though originally spurred by Shakespeare's words and ideas, the results must be different because of the passage of time and the vicissitudes of taste.

Since there is no 'tradition', the exhortation to 'stick to the tradition' has to be seen for what it is: a veiled objection to the manner and nature of modern adaptations. What is the alternative? To let Shakespeare speak for himself! Again, an impossibility, because, even if one forsakes theatrical presentation of his works and leaves him to the study (where so many academics would prefer him to be), each reader's subjectivity is mentally staging works of their own. Strictly speaking, there is no way of determining Shakespeare without reference to the minds of actors, directors, designers and scholars through whom he is being metamorphosed. This is a great relief. It means that the only 'tradition' we really know is the recent past – the last hundred to one hundred and fifty years. From our reading of that period, we know that the 'tradition' was as multifarious as the hundred or so years that preceded it. By consulting the tradition, we are granted the freedom to dispense with it.

But often 'tradition' is used as a synonym for 'historicity' and what people really mean is: if Shakespeare dealt with the Wars of the Roses or the Renaissance, we should not juxtapose the First World War or the period of 'flower power'. Which brings us back to the former question of how much liberty we can allow ourselves with these works, and the answer: that all freedom, in art as in life, is umbilically connected to responsibility. If we can make ourselves responsible for preserving what is essential and unalterable in the works of William Shakespeare, we can exercise the freedom to interpolate and digress as we choose.

6. The way to show our appreciation for Shakespeare is to stage him as often as possible

The way to show our appreciation for Shakespeare is to recognise our inadequacy in mounting him properly. To remove that inadequacy, our efforts should be aimed at creating first-class acting ensembles which are permanent and can develop with continuity. Through enlightened training of actors and education of directors, we should learn how to play the verse and fulfil the demands of the plays, instead of dutifully reviving them in conditions that only emphasise our artistic and intellectual shortcomings.

7. Shakespeare will never die

Just as we all have gruelling memories of Shakespeare being shoved down our throats in high school and of having to overcome the tedium and non-comprehension of works which we later came to realise were rich and fecund, so the danger exists that mindless iterations of the plays by unqualified practitioners and misguided zealots may turn off audiences permanently. There is one theory that Shakespeare is always box office poison. There is another that he is always sure-fire. The truth is that vigorous, imaginative and well-played Shakespeare confirms the positive opinion many people have of the Bard. Sloppy, puerile and confused productions confirm the opposite theory: that his greatness has been exaggerated and that, if he belongs anywhere, it is in the study and the library. It was Jean-Louis Barrault who said that one must respect what one presumes to love. To respect Shakespeare is to confront, critically and without illusion, the poverty of our skills in realising his work in any sweeping, national way and to make practical efforts – both artistically and in terms of grants and subsidies – to remedy our deficiencies.

Coriolanus

12 incorporated

Shortly after the Irangate hearings in Washington, and immediately before the presidential election of 1988, the Old Globe Theatre in San Diego presented a modern-dress production of *Coriolanus* in an adaptation by John Hirsch. In many ways, this was a typically American exercise in Shakespearian revisionism, the likes of which one might encounter in Stratford, Connecticut, the New York Shakespeare Festival or, for that matter, England's National Theatre. This was Shakespeare up-dated, transplanted geographically (from Rome to Washington DC and Nicaragua), the text interpolated with colloquial additions and the whole posture altered so as to be contemporaneous with recent events. In short, the kind of production that causes seizures among the purists and transports of delight among those who like their classics liberally spiced up.

Being an intelligent and well-directed production (John Hirsch was also the director), it struck me as a useful test case for the jazzifications of Shakespeare which, more and more, take place on American and European stages, and I am considering it here not so much for its own sake, but as an example of what happens when the parameters of Shakespeare's works are extended (some would contend, contracted) to accommodate fresh ideas.

The play's central character, no longer a Roman warrior but now a bemedalled Marine officer redolent of Oliver North, is seen triumphant in battles against a (presumably) Central American force resembling the Sandinistas. Back from the wars, Coriolanus is fêted at the Capitol and primed for a position of supreme leadership, the Senate and the political Establishment clearly bent on exploiting his military victory for the furtherance of their own national aims. Volumnia, the hero's mother, here consigned to a wheelchair, is a kind of crippled Washington matriarch; Virgilia, a doting, suburban wife who,

Jackie Kennedy-like, clasps her tiny children to her and lends conspicuous support to her lauded, warrior–husband at all public occasions. Coriolanus himself, suffused with his traditional pride, is a surly tool of the state of which he is an integral part.

For the first five minutes of the performance, you find yourself recoiling from the slack diction, the prosaic interpolations and the gratutious switch of period; but, as the evening progresses, the consistency of Hirsch's vision and a highly-disciplined *mise-en-scène* persuades us that this is as legitimate an approach as any other. And even as some part of our higher intellect registers objections to the portrayal of Menenius Agrippa as a kind of wily Huey Long with a Southern drawl, and Coriolanus as a gung-ho, super-patriot, the conviction behind the acting and the audacity behind the conception gradually wins us over.

There is no disputing the fact that the verse was gabbled and the nuances of Shakespeare's text became the first casualties of Hirsch's guerilla tactics against the play but then, if one exchanges Plutarch for the Pentagon and swords for sub-machine-guns, there is a kind of logic in prosifying, even coarsening, Shakespeare's strict verse patterns. The verbal interpolations (colloquial military epithets mixed with lowbrow slang) sounded like gross actor-improvs (which is probably what they were) and clashed harshly with what we heard and comprehended of the original; but it was often a salutary clash, producing a novel, theatrical *frisson* in the midst of a play which, approached in too august terms, often delivers considerably less than its author's grand design.

Hirsch used a bank of video monitors as a kind of Greek chorus to comment on the transplanted Roman action and there were regular news updates describing the progress of the war, as well as commercials promoting Coriolanus's victories. We began to experience the action through the media – the way we do most modern guerilla wars.

At first, it was as if the performance were a pungent news programme being superimposed upon a classical selection from a BBC Prom concert and, eventually, with the insistent static of two stations competing for the same air-wave, the listener ultimately had to opt for one or the other. For those who opted for Shakespeare Pure, this *Coriolanus* appeared as nothing more than a noisome intrusion, a travesty of the original, but, for those prepared to accept Hirsch's harsh metaphors and transplanted settings, the play came through with a new kind of clarity and excitement – derived directly from the switch into a more immediate, more recognisable social framework.

As the evening progressed, one became aware that the parallels simply did not jibe. Coriolanus suffers from hubris and is an unapproachable patrician who despises the mob. Oliver North suffers from misguided chauvinism, is the darling of the plebs and, had he wanted to, could have knocked George Bush off the Republican ticket in 1988 and written his own. The tension between Coriolanus and Aufidius, here dramatised as a rivalry between an American military commander and a Central American guerilla chieftain, had no immediate contemporary parallel. North was not an active combatant, but an inside facilitator for right-wing American power blocs. North's nemesis was not really the Sandinistas, it was the United States Congress, to whom he lied out of a corrupted sense of anti-communist fervour. There is no character in Shakespeare's play who can 'stand in' for President Ronald Reagan, for whom North was a 'patriot' and at whose behest he committed acts which caused him to run foul of the law. The pieces of the 'conception' and the political events on which they are based refused to marry up. However, during the course of the evening, the actual events were replaced by those in Shakespeare's play and, despite jolting contradictions here and there, we came to accept the Marine hero, the senators and the politicians merely as surrogates for the original characters in Shakespeare's tragedy. That is, we came to experience Shakespeare's play through the glass proffered by the director/adaptor and, consciously or unconsciously, made allowances for the discrepancies – as, I would imagine, allowances were made for Orson Welles's Fascist-dress version of *Julius Caesar* in the thirties, where again, the 'parallels' did not exactly fit, but were close enough for one story to inform the other.

At the end of the performance there was a funny kind of blur between the play and, as it were, the play-*upon*-the-play. We had an experience which was in part Shakespearian and in part documentary. We were told a story of a patrician Roman general who ran foul of a populace which would have liked to embrace him, and another story about a soldier who, reprimanded for his conduct in battle, refused to accept the egregious connotations placed upon it. We were given, in unequal portions, a wadge of Roman history and a slice of political current events. We were in Rome and in Washington. In Antium and Nicaragua. In a theatre and in a television studio. In the past and in the present.

What, ultimately, were the advantages of Hirsch's imposition upon Shakespeare's *Coriolanus?* He 'translated' Shakespeare's Roman events into recent political events which, because of their notoriety and political impact, added another dimension to the material. This new 'dimension' contained a number of attitudes and feelings to the play, without which we would have had to rely on traditional and historical reconstructions. The production's modernism brought with it a whole slew of emotions which, strictly speaking, do not belong to *Coriolanus* but which, nevertheless, augment the original story and secrete potent dramatic overtones. Many Americans felt strongly about Oliver North; about Reagan's frustrated attempts to aid the Contras; about the political implications of intercession in Central America. Irrelevant as all these 'feelings' might be to Shakespeare's original design, they were activated by Hirsch's scenario and mingled with that other set of emotions generated by the original Roman subject. Two sets of feelings began to work simultaneously – those generated by Shakespeare's story and those superimposed by the contemporary parallels.

One could argue that one set of feelings cancelled out the other, and that the price Hirsch paid for introducing arbitrary elements was to weaken and divert the stronger ones already contained in Shakespeare's play. Having created a paradigm composed of Nicaragua, the Pentagon and Oliver North, there is some part of the audience's psychology which expects a pay-off to these new narrative strands, and, since the original play effectively dismantled them as it went along, there was a sharp sense of frustration. Towards the end, if we were engrossed at all, it was in Shakespearian considerations: will Volumnia be able to persuade Coriolanus to forsake the Volscians and avoid the ruin of Rome? How will Aufidius deal with Coriolanus's betrayal? Questions very far removed from the implications of Oliver North's behaviour at the Senate hearings, or the fate of the Contras in light of the government's refusal to underwrite aid.

Ultimately one asks, what in fact was *paralleled* here? And the answer is: personality types and vague resemblances between Roman action and recent American events! And what caused the parallels to break down? Personality types and vague resemblances between Roman action and recent American events! But another question is begged: did the emotional accretions of the new information in any way help the telling of the original story? As much as one is inclined to say that they did not – that one was at odds with the other – the palpable fact is that they did. Because one was able to identify Coriolanus with a contemporary figure about whom most people held strong opinions, a dimension was added to the Shakespearian experience which, in a 'classical' version of the play, would not have emerged. Weighing the value of that new dimension against the dilution of the play's original premises throws one into a quandary. It is true that a marvellously performed, traditional version of Shakespeare's *Coriolanus* might well have produced *reverberations* of recent historical events and, at the same time, maintained the integrity of the play's original intentions. But would it have been able to harness the strong feelings generated by these specific parallels? Is it not more likely that we would have lost a certain political dimension by being visually restricted to the ancient Roman milieu?

In Gunter Grass's *The Plebeians Rehearse the Uprising*, *Coriolanus*, or rather Brecht's Marxist rescension of the play, is also used as a framework for a different dramatic experience. In Brecht's rendering, Shakespeare's hero is depicted as an enemy of the working class and his 'pride' is seen as a tragic flaw which the social consciousness of the plebeians indicts and opposes. 'Brecht,' writes Grass in his introduction, 'reduces his Coriolan to the level of an efficient specialist, who, though useful in time of war, oversteps his functions in peacetime and is therefore dismissed by the people and its elected tribunes ... Brecht's Coriolan is swept aside because he behaves like a reactionary and fails to understand the sign of the times, the springtime of the young Roman Republic.'

In Grass's play, we are at two removes from Shakespeare. He has composed his play to indict Brecht himself who, during the uprising of June 1953, 'did not interrupt his rehearsals' to provide support for the protesting workers soon to be mowed down by the Soviet tanks and the East German police. Grass's concern is not so much the ambiguous nature of Shakespeare's character, but of Brecht himself – the 'poet of the masses' who at the height of the workers' rebellion in East Germany ended a letter addressed to Ulbricht, the Soviet High Commissioner in Germany and the Premier of the German Democratic Republic, with the words: 'At this moment I feel the need to express my solidarity with the Socialist Unity Party of Germany.'

Brecht's re-angling of *Coriolanus* was an overt attempt to bring a modern political consciousness to bear on a play which, in its original form, sidestepped an issue which, historically speaking, could not have occurred to Shakespeare: a ploy similar to that in *Trumpets and Drums*, his rewrite of Farquhar's *The Recruiting Officer*. In both works, Brecht, the revisionist, legitimately stakes out a classic and proceeds both to rethink and re-angle it according to his own political lights; a thoroughly legitimate activity among contemporary playwrights and directors. But in Hirsch's case, which is the case of many contemporary directors, the revisionism is imposed on the classical text in the form of external change, in the hope that new implications will banish those of the original. When Brecht re-orders Shakespeare or Farquhar or Marlowe for his own purposes, he is unequivocally indicating that he wishes to alter the plays' original ideology. He clearly has another ideology to put in their place and he is using the plays' received ideas as jumping-off points for new statements or implications. In so doing, he is deliberately tinkering with the original organism in order to produce another. But when directors without Brecht's intellectual gifts approach a classic and merely douse it with alien ideas in the hope that their paint job will obliterate the original, the effect is often that the new gloss merely calls attention to the undercoat.

In Shakespearian reinterpretation, there are basically two angles of attack: the Frontal Assault or the Subversion From Within. In the case of the former, it is sometimes possible to produce a startling sense of disorientation by which two sets of antithetical ideas cohabit the same work of art. The success of that mix depends on the relevance of the new ideas to the original and, to an even greater extent, how much of the original play is revitalised by the infusion of those ideas. In the case of the Subversion From Within, the engine of the original play is actually restructured, its original ideas rerouted, to arrive at a completely new terminus – and, usually, one the author never intended. The second approach almost always demands textual liberties, revisions and the incorporation of new material. But in both cases the thematic implications of the original work are both feeding and being conditioned by the insertion of new material – which is why, ultimately, the experiment is intrinsically Shakespearian, since, without the stance and cast of the original play, the rescension would be unthinkable.

Contrasted with these approaches, there is the practice of merely bouncing a work off the surface of the original classic, as, for instance, *Kiss Me Kate* is bounced off *The Taming of the*

Shrew, or *West Side Story* off *Romeo and Juliet*, or *Rosencrantz and Guildenstern Are Dead* off *Hamlet*. In these instances, Shakespeare functions merely as a source for new works, in much the same way that Greek, Roman and medieval sources served to propel Shakespeare into works only tangentially related to his own plays. The link here is tenuous and the cultural sovereignty of the new work is largely independent of the work on which it is based – so much so that audiences can appreciate the former with virtually no knowledge of the latter.

For the past two hundred years or so, we have experienced a variety of frontal assaults on Shakespeare's works and, today, we are very accustomed to the torrents of new wine being poured into the old bottles. But internal subversions of the plays are much less common and much less acceptable, perhaps because they require an ingenuity and mechanism every bit as sophisticated as the one they appear to be replacing. In many ways, Brecht has come closest, because he accepted the authority of Shakespeare's original work and challenged the author on an equal level of discourse. Of course, for many, Brecht's partisanship is a constantly diminishing factor in his adaptations. In most cases, Shakespeare is whittled down for the sake of an arbitrary reading and no amount of clever political engineering can atone for the loss of poetic complexity. But, nevertheless, in Brecht, the principle is sound. If you want the classic to mean something else, you do not merely *intone* it differently, you dig into its innards and transform its basic constituents.

The biggest, wettest and scaliest of all red herrings is the charge that this is distorting the originals. In a sense, the originals exist *in order to be* distorted. The practice of all modern art involves the twisting of traditional materials – distortion is part of the modern painter's means of expression – just as dissonance is part of the musician's and contrapuntal movement part of the dancer's. The real nemesis of Shakespearian reinterpretation is the crudity and banality of so many of those 'new ideas' being foisted onto the originals. Painting a moustache on the Mona Lisa is a good once-only joke, but if Duchamp had proceeded to give Little Boy Blue a pecker or Rembrandt's Self-Portrait a blackeye we would quickly tire of the effrontery. In the case of most classical directors, a theme of crippling obviousness is grafted onto plays which are models of enthralling complexity, thereby proclaiming the intellectual paucity of the innovations. If the creation of heavyweight blank verse drama involves herculean skills of composition, harder still is the accretion of new dramatic ideas to augment and enliven the effect of the original. And this is because, in many cases, the deeper import of Shakespeare's original plays is not clearly understood or only partially unearthed. As Jan Kott says elsewhere in this book, there are certain plays which at certain times *become* contemporary – because of a confluence between recent events and past history. When, at such times, a classic stands at the crossroads, it opens up a third way for a play to go. That happened during the occupation of France in the case of Jean Anouilh's *Antigone*; it happened again during Olivier's *Henry V* in wartime England. It tends to happen every so often when a modern sensibility connects or counteracts with a great play of the past, and, when it does, we talk about a classic being 'revitalised'. In the future, it may more often take the form of encountering a classic with a completely new physiognomy and an entirely different kind of diction – remembering what it used to look and sound like, and appreciating the radical changes it has undergone.

Privatising
13 *Julius Caesar*

In the old days, politics took place on the stump – at the Forum or the Capitol, in public squares, market-places, at outdoor rallies, on whistlestops – wherever the politicians felt they could count on the populace to gather. But, since the advent of radio, and certainly since the growth of television, the site for most political gatherings has been the living-room. In the radiophonic thirties political oratory gave way to the fireside chat and, in the sixties and seventies, televised debates. Gradually, oratory dwindled into chit-chat, and rhetoric into glittering generalities.

Although *Julius Caesar* was conceived as an epic for the great outdoors, the change in political custom has made it difficult to recreate the ambiance chronicled by Plutarch and dramatised by Shakespeare. And, in some ways, the grandiose approach to this tragedy runs counter to the temperament of the piece, for despite its Capitol settings and its sense of crowds-in-motion, it has the makings of an intimate drama, almost a chamber play. Even as it stands, some of its most crucial scenes are played out in intimate surroundings – in Brutus's orchard, in Caesar's sleeping-quarters, inside Brutus's tent, a room in Antony's house, and so on. But, more significantly, the expression of many of its crucial ideas happen between two or three characters in pressured interpersonal exchanges, away from the thunder of battle or the sweep of the Senate. At the core of the historical grandeur which is, in some ways, only the play's facade, there are a few vital, self-contained, intimate scenes between characters who, in unburdening themselves in moments of poignant, psychological revelation, deliver the essence of the piece.

I do not contend that a large stage and a cast of thousands cannot make *Julius Caesar* an exciting spectacle, but without giving those telling private moments their full value, the play can easily become a windy simulacrum of an overblown historical event and blur what lies at its centre – that is, the exploration of tangled, contradictory motives and the unravelling of moral ambiguities.

From its first scenes, through the conspiracy and right up to the assassination of Caesar, the play has an inexorable forward motion. It takes on a second wind at the Forum, where Brutus must justify and Antony question the murder of Caesar. By the time we have reached the end of Act III, Shakespeare has shot his bolt. His most magnificent and most pliant character, the Roman citizenry, has been wooed, swayed and politicised, and from that point on there is something fated and creaky about the battle scenes, the quarrel between Cassius and Brutus, the predictable twinges of remorse that haunt Brutus through Sardis and Phillipi and finally bring about his noble demise. It is as if the inner conflict of his main character, Shakespeare's starting point for the play, was obliged to yield to the *données* of the action scenes and, like the scriptwriter imprisoned by the officially-approved outline, he was honour-bound to fulfil the obligatory requirements of a prescribed narrative.

The most dramatic strand in *Julius Caesar* is not the icono-graphic assassination, the ensuing battles and the spiral of Brutus's tormented downfall, but the almost contemporary ambivalence that a liberal sensibility experiences when con-fronted with real or imagined abuse of power and how that sensibility wavers in the face of a moral dilemma which insists it come down on one side or the other. In *Caesar*, more perhaps than in any other work, Shakespeare has dramatised the choice of evils and the agonies involved in making such choices.

It could be argued that the genius of Caesar destroyed the republic, but also that the benefits of his dictatorship outweighed the evils which preceded and followed his reign. Shakespeare alludes to Caesar's failings, but they are indicted only through hearsay – that is, in the unconvincing and partisan diatribe of Marullus, boosting Pompey and putting down Caesar, and by Cassius, whose personal axe grinds so loudly it forces us to question his objectivity. Apart from a certain imperiousness in his nature (after all, this *is* Caesar), the Emperor personifies none of the evils we associate with Shakespeare's historical villains. There is no trace of The Duke of Gloucester about him, or even of Claudius. If he has some of Coriolanus's hubris, it is far more justified in Caesar than it is in Caius Marcius. As for Cassius's shortcomings – envy, pride, thwarted ambition – they are clearly delineated in the character of the man and there for all to see. But Brutus's imperfections are almost lovingly etched, as if the author were saying: I know these may be thought of as faults but, for the life of me, I cannot dislike them. And, although Shakespeare is obliged to punish the character for his actions, he does so with palpable reluctance. Right up to the end, when Brutus is permitted a patrician's death and, in the last moments of the play, eulogised by Antony as 'the noblest Roman of them all', Brutus, like Hamlet, is, for all his faults, lovingly fondled by the author.

And what was it that Shakespeare so loved in Brutus? Why, his weakness, his moral impediments, his adorable character imperfections – the same qualities that made him enamoured of Hamlet, Coriolanus and Richard II, his irresistible 'feminine' heroes. It is almost as if a protagonist had to suffer some fundamental weakness of character in order to warrant Shakespeare's full interest and sympathy and, of all of them, Brutus is, in many ways, the most vulnerable, the most flawed, the most disaster-prone.

Like Trotsky (whom he strongly brings to mind), his political acumen is consistently subverted by his intellect and convoluted moral sense. After Lenin's death, while Trotsky was debating the dialectics of the revolution, Stalin was organising its rank and file for the succession. Trotsky, in his writings and in his speeches, assumed there was some invisible tribunal which would arbitrate the burning questions raised by the revolution. Stalin knew there was no such tribunal; that, in fact, the only tribunals that mattered were the ones he constructed himself and staffed with intimidated underlings. Trotsky thought power emanated from principle; Stalin knew that power determined principle and that, in the long run, if you had power, you could quite easily get along without principles at all.

The misguided zealot, the poet–statesman, is one strain in Brutus's fluffy personality; the other is the paralysed liberal. If Trotsky can be found in his make-up, there is more than a little trace of Adlai Stevenson as well. There has always been a breed of statesman that has confused liberal convictions with political efficacy, who felt that one could give birth to the other, guide the other, make the other the engine of the former's purpose. It is not that Cassius is more ruthless or less principled than Brutus, but, unlike Brutus, he has been able to make that division between principle and power which is perhaps the most important lesson any politician ever learns. Cassius is prepared to break eggs to make omelettes, while Brutus will debate the whole question of dairy products as opposed to carnivorousness. It is the kind of fine-lined reasonableness which is antithetical to practical political ends and which accounts for the rejection, in America, of people such as George McGovern, Hubert Humphrey and Adlai Stevenson – just as it explains the elections of people such as John F. Kennedy, Richard Nixon and Ronald Reagan. It is this same effete liberalism, this obtuseness in the face of self-evident realities, which also accounts for Brutus's military bungling and his fatal indiscretion in allowing Antony to speak at Caesar's funeral. Anyone so hopelessly imprisoned by the super-ego can have no real knowledge of the treacheries that confront the id.

At the core of Brutus's woolly-mindedness is the same kind of flaccidity one often discerns in Shakespeare himself. In the words of Granville-Barker, the playwright 'had preserved, we may say, for use at need, his actor's gift of making effective things he did not fully understand': a quality most apparent in many of Shakespeare's histories where, in a sense, his eloquence runs before his intelligence. For the only real motive he gives Brutus in the dispatch of Caesar is his ambition; that is to say, his proclivity towards corruptibility and future misuse of power. (Although, had he wanted to, there was sufficient historical evidence available to paint Caesar much blacker: the bribery, the corruption, the arrogance in office.) But Shakespeare does not posit these flaws. Caesar is to be punished for a *potentiality* in his character rather than for any manifest evil. This, as Maccallum points out, would never wash with the ancient Roman and only barely washes today. 'It would never have occurred to the genuine republican of olden time that any justification was needed for dispatching a man who sought to usurp the sovereign place; and if it had, this is certainly the last justification that would have entered his head.' But it is the one that most appeals to Shakespeare, because it is rooted in that flaw in Brutus's personality which, perhaps because it corresponds to a frailty in his own nature, the author finds most endearing.

The private nature of the play is constantly subverting its public face. Even in the Forum scenes, which are arguably the most public in the play, one encounters the sort of intimacy one associates with private services rather than state funerals. Antony's peroration, despite the punctuations of the citizenry, is throbbingly personal ('You all do know this mantle: I remember / The first time ever Caesar put it on / 'Twas on a summer's evening, in his tent / That day he overcame the Nervii.') And the reading of the will itself, in order to produce the intended incendiary effect, depends on a kind of sustained poignancy. Try as he does for historical distance and the Grand Design, the personal, the intimate, the sentimental weaves its way into Shakespeare's material.

Of all the character ambiguities in *Julius Caesar*, the one that envelops Antony is perhaps the greatest. Dismissed by Brutus as a mere appendage of Caesar and generally downgraded by the other conspirators, Antony has his finest moments before the corpse of the bloody emperor and then, in some captivating bursts of demogoguery, at the funeral oration. Indeed, after that scene, it is as if Antony is being vaunted as a worthy moral antagonist to Brutus, but it is a hard-nosed, ruthless Antony who, in concert with Octavius, routinely 'pricks' off names on the post-revolutionary hit-list and then devotes twenty-two lines to abusing Aemilius Lepidus as a useless packhorse and flunkey. Even Antony's hands-down success at the funeral appears to be rooted in his own identification with the common man's mentality.

It is this post-revolutionary Antony who tempts us to reassess the clever orator in the funeral scene (who, incidentally, saves his most treacherous stratagems until after Brutus and the others have left). Ultimately, despite the eloquence of his arguments and the vigour of his loyalty to the dead Caesar, one concludes that, probably, he *was* only an appendage to the emperor and his vindictiveness against Brutus and the rest stems from the fact that he has been made redundant by Caesar's fall. It then seems like the most natural thing in the world to throw in with the rival force and do what he can to oust the usurpers – although, throughout, his own morality appears to be cut from the same cloth as Caesar's, and so our sympathy for him remains grudging.

There is about Antony that whiff of the careerist–politician which one finds in the most contemptible members of local government – a kind of GLC mentality which, writ large, produces the exalted toadies and back-room boys of national politics as well. Antony has fallen into a cushy job which provides convenient perks, an unlimited expense account and an ability to indulge in the debauchery that we know will eventually consume him. As is often the case in Shakespeare, our most apparent heroes not only have feet of clay but, as in the case of Antony, hearts of flint as well. All of which, despite the rout of the funeral scene, tends to add dimensionality to Brutus and strengthen the rationale behind the assassination. It is both fit, proper and utterly predictable that Antony, the George Jessell of the Forum set, will have the last words on Brutus's death. It is the inveterate stooge and subaltern who can most readily assess the worth of a man such as Brutus and conclude: 'His life was gentle, and the elements / So mixed in him that Nature might stand up / And say to all the world, "This was a man!"' No such sentiments could be expressed at Antony's demise.

The women in *Julius Caesar* get very short shrift. Essentially, Portia and Calpurnia are involved in almost identical actions, the former trying to persuade her husband to divulge the subject of his nocturnal preoccupations and the latter trying, on the basis of her female intuition, to persuade *her* husband to cancel a visit to the Capitol. In reality, Portia is trying to prevent Brutus's treachery, just as Calpurnia is trying to avoid the conspirator's treachery against Caesar: two loving and concerned women trying to reverse the irreversible juggernaut of history. And when both their husbands are felled by their respective fates, neither is around to offer consolation. Portia, mentally punished by Brutus's absence in the war and fearful of the counter-insurrection against him, falls 'distract' and swallows fire. After Caesar's assassination, although Antony delivers a touching peroration ('O, pardon me thou bleeding piece of earth'), Calpurnia is not permitted a word – not even at the funeral ceremony. The absence of the wives' involvement in their husbands' fortunes is understandable, given the public (that is, epic) nature of the play, and yet, if a way had been found to provide these missing dimensions, some of the play's humanity – implied but neglected – would have added missing fibre.

It is curious, in the case of Portia, that her chief rival for Brutus's affections seems to be Cassius, who positively has a crush on Brutus and, in the Tent Scene, reacts like the spurned lover he, in one sense, is. The tenderest sentiments towards Brutus are expressed not by Portia but by Cassius ('I have not from your eyes that gentleness / And show of love as I was wont to have.') and whereas, after the conspiracy scene, Brutus merely wants to get Portia to go to bed, he deals with Cassius's rejection as if he owed it some more fundamental concern. I do not intend to suggest a homosexual overtone here, as I do not think one exists – other than the macho homosexuality that one finds in all Shakespeare's antique characters, and which was embedded in Greek and Roman societies as much as it was in Elizabethan life. But the suggestion of homosexuality is especially strong in *Caesar* particularly in those furtive last scenes where Brutus is trying to get first Clitus then Strato to hold the sword on which he will take his life. There is something almost perverse (masturbatory even) about Brutus's attempts to enlist the aid of those unwilling soldiers in his final surcease. In death, as in life, the soldier needs his loyal comrades in order to discharge himself nobly. The sexual undertones in these scenes are echoed by Brutus's own ambivalence towards Caesar when he admits: 'I have no personal cause to spurn at him, but for the general' and even Antony concedes that Brutus was 'Caesar's angel'. ('Judge O, you gods, how dearly Caesar loved him!') The final stanza of Wilde's *Ballad of Reading Gaol* suddenly seems very apt here.

> All men kill the thing they love,
> By all let this be heard,
> Some do it with a bitter look,
> Some with a flattering word,
> The coward does it with a kiss,
> The brave man with a sword!

Brutus's love of Caesar is corrupted with fear for the thing he might become – just as Cassius's love of Brutus is corrupted with envy of the nobility he does not possess. As in ancient tribal societies, weaker characters try to appropriate those qualities they covet through ritual murder.

In the Red-baiting, subversive thirties and then again in the witch-hunting McCarthyite fifties, the scene with Cinna the poet always seemed like an epigraph for the times. Here was the Dies Committee or House Un-American Activities Committee hounding some poor innocent who happened to have the same name as a pinko or fellow-traveller or was listed, entirely by mistake, in a copy of *Red Channels*. Cinna is every well-meaning, innocent bystander who gets crushed – not only by the spite of Fascist dictatorship, but also by the totalitarian tendency that frequently overruns democracies. In a straightforward political rendering of the play, it is a crucial vignette, and even in Shakespeare it seems like a ghoulishly prophetic little addendum – brilliantly extra-polated from a single sentence in Suetonius describing the events following Caesar's assassination. Why introduce a poor, innocent poet being tortured by vengeful plebeians, when the great sweep of your action has to do with imposing historical personages and profound dialectical argument? I guess the only answer is that the author's infallible canniness felt the need to demonstrate one of the ways in which 'A curse shall light upon the limbs of men / Domestic fury and fierce civil strife / Shall cumber all the parts of Italy'. Whatever the cause, it is one of those brilliant touches by which we unquestionably recognise a master's hand.

However, in a non-political version of the play, it needs to be reassessed, even rejigged. For Brutus, experiencing that 'phan-tasma' or 'hideous dream' engendered by his actions, it is not too much of a stretch to imagine the chief conspirator visualising the kind of punishment being meted out by those loyal to the regime against the perpetrators of that heinous crime. It may be argued that the transposition of such a scene from one character to another is a gross violation of the author's intent, but what seems to me indisputable is that the object of that scene – to portray, in a small-scale, naturalistic episode, the unforeseen consequences of great men's politically-motivated actions – can be conveyed in any number of ways, one of these being juxtaposition. Cinna is, after all a poet. So is Brutus. His sensitivity in the contemplation of Caesar's assassination is very different from that of the other assassins. He has the ability to contemplate not only its public-relations consequences, but the impact of its imagery in cen-turies to come. It is Brutus's imaginative grasp of the social and moral complexities of totalitarian rule which motors the entire action of the play. If, as has often been said, he is a 'philosopher', it is in the same sense as Coleridge or Milton, Wordsworth or Shelley.

The subtext of the Tent Scene has always been ambiguous. Cassius rails at Brutus because he comes to the defence of a man who has taken bribes – which turns Brutus's wrath on Cassius who, he tells us, is 'also much condemned to have an itching palm' – although, a moment later, he rails at Cassius because he refused him money to pay his legions which Brutus had not the temerity to exact 'from the hands of peasants ... by any indirection'. Which seems to suggest that the dubious methods by which Cassius appropriated money were irrelevant, so long as Brutus himself did not have to lower himself to adopt them. Brutus's palm was just as itchy as Cassius's but he deigned not to scratch it himself, although he had no compunction about it being scratched by his fellow-soldier.

But finances notwithstanding, the ambivalence of the scene stems from the fact that it feels like a tiff between lovers or an old married couple who, no sooner having vented their hostility on some insignificant subject, proceed to make it up and, in so doing, reveal that something much deeper was behind it all. From a psychological standpoint, there is no question that the sources of Brutus's irritation in the scene is not so much Cassius's mercenariness as the strain on his stoic nature imposed by the news of Portia's death. Indeed, no sooner has his aggression been released than Brutus admits as much: 'O, Cassius, I am sick of many griefs ... No man bears sorrow better. Portia is dead.' In recognition of the true cause of Brutus's anger, Cassius, reconsidering their squabble, cries out: 'How 'scaped I killing when I crossed you so? O insupportable and touching loss!' In other words, had he known Portia was the underlying cause of Brutus's aggravation, he would never have dwelt on the paltry subject of money. As in the early scenes of the play, Brutus mingles his feelings towards Portia with those of Cassius and it seems that, every time he feels a pang of marital guilt, he is obliged to placate Cassius's passionate feeings towards him.

No doubt the ambidextrous sexual conduct of Roman society is the underlying reason for all these ambivalences (even Caesar was suspected of homosexual relations with King Nicomedes) but, in our own time, there are enough emotional parallels in the scene for them to be appropriated for other uses. What concerned me in restructuring *Caesar* was how much of Brutus's love for Portia got diverted into his political mission; how much of it was shared or transposed in his relations with Cassius and members of the Senate; how much of it, inspired by Caesar, had to be denied or sublimated in order for him to remain 'the noblest Roman of them all'.

Brutus, like Hamlet or Macbeth or Richard II – all characters involved in struggles against their nature – is the victim of a tortured subjectivity.

> Between the acting of a dreadful thing
> And the first motion, all the interim is
> Like a phantasma or a hideous dream.
> The genius and the mortal instruments
> Are then in council, and the state of man,
> Like to a little kingdom, suffers then
> The nature of an insurrection.

The words, though Brutus's, could serve just as well for Macbeth – even for Gloucester at Bosworth Field. It is this 'insurrection' which, it seems to me, is central to Shakespeare's purpose, albeit diverted by the 'cover story' of Julius Caesar, the Plutarchian chronicle, the Elizabethan consciousness of Caesar's world straddling greatness and the rest. It is as if the story Shakespeare set out to tell – that is, the intense moral pressures that beset and eventually destroy a man juggling the paradox of individual conscience and collective good – was too diversionary to be contained in an epic dealing with the greatest emperor of all time. Here was a vast canvas sprawled out in front of the author, full of battles, factionalism and overwhelming historical events, and, alongside it, his desire to use only a small portion of it for a taut, psychological tale about moral contradiction. Part of him, using thin and delicate pen-and-ink strokes, drew out the story he felt impelled to tell, and then another part of him, picking up a bloody great paintbrush, filled in the rest of the canvas. That which is epic and grandiose in *Julius Caesar* seems to run against the grain of what is private and psychological. It is no accident that Julius Caesar seems to be almost an interloper in the play that bears his name. He does not really live or function in the same atmosphere which contains Brutus. And that is because one is a personification of a myth that could not yet be dealt with in realistic terms, and the other a tortured sensibility very much like those Shakespeare had already created earlier and would develop further a few years later, and with whom he had the strongest empathy. That the two were yoked together by the commercial needs of the time should not blind us to the fact that *Julius Caesar* is a highly schizoid work and one which can be divided one way or the other.

• Julius Caesar freely adapted by Charles Marowitz

•

A playing-space.

Hanging from above, like old battle relics, a set of thunder-sheets. In the centre, a great gong. On the sides, smaller gongs and bells.

In the darkness, we hear:

ALL: [whispered]:   Beware the ides of March.

[*LIGHTS UP. CAESAR CENTRE; all others in semi-circle around him.*]

CAESAR: What man is that?

CASSIUS: A soothsayer bids you beware the ides of March.

CAESAR: Set him before me; let me see his face.

CASCA: Fellow, come from the throng; look upon Caesar.

[*BRUTUS is brought forward from the group to confront CAESAR.*]

CAESAR: What say'st thou to me now? Speak once again.

[*BRUTUS is silent as the SOOTHSAYER, from his place, says:*]

SOOTHSAYER: Beware the ides of March.

CAESAR [*TO BRUTUS*]:   The ides of March are come.

SOOTHSAYER: Ay, Caesar, but not gone.

CAESAR [*Looks BRUTUS square in the face for a long while*]:   He is a dreamer; let us leave him.

[*BRUTUS returns to his place. The senate forms for its session.*]

Are we all ready? What is now amiss

That Caesar and his Senate must redress?

METELLUS CIMBER: Most high, most mighty, and most puissant Caesar,

Metellus Cimber throws before thy seat

An humble heart.

CAESAR: I must prevent thee, Cimber

These couchings and these lowly courtesies

Might fire the blood of ordinary men

And turn preordinance and first decree

Into the law of children. Be not fond

To think that Caesar bears such rebel blood

That will be thawed from the true quality

With that which melteth fools – I mean, sweet words,

Low crooked curtsies, and base spaniel fawning.

Thy brother by decree is banished.

If thou dost bend and pray and fawn for him,

I spurn thee like a cur out of my way.

Know, Caesar doth not wrong, nor without cause

Will he be satisfied.

METELLUS CIMBER: Is there no voice more worthy than my own
    To sound more sweetly in great Caesar's ear
    For the repealing of my banished brother?
BRUTUS [*Kneeling*]:   I kiss thy hand, but not in flattery Caesar,
    Desiring thee that Publius Cimber may
    Have an immediate freedom of repeal.
[*Portia steps forward to take the kneeling Brutus's hand* ... CUT
INTO NEW SCENE.]
PORTIA: Brutus, my lord!
BRUTUS: Portia! What mean you? Wherefore rise you now?
    It is not for your health to commit
    Your weak condition to the raw cold morning.
PORTIA: Nor for yours neither. Y'have urgently, Brutus,
    Stole from my bed. And yesternight at supper
    You suddenly arose and walked about,
    Musing and sighing with your arms across;
    And when I asked you what the matter was,
    You stared upon me with ungentle looks.
    It will not let you eat nor talk nor sleep,
    And could it work so much upon your shape,
    As it hath much prevailed on your condition,
    I should not know you Brutus. Dear, my lord,
    Make me acquainted with your cause of grief.
BRUTUS: I am not well in health, and that is all.
CASSIUS: I have not from your eyes that gentleness
    And show of love as I was wont to have.
    You bear too stubborn and too strange a hand
    Over your friend that loves you.
BRUTUS: Cassius, Be not deceived. I have veiled my look,
    I turn the trouble of my countenance
    Merely upon myself. [*To* PORTIA]
    I am not well in health, and that is all.
PORTIA: Brutus is wise and, were he not in health,
    He would embrace the means to come by it.
BRUTUS: Why so I do.
    [*To* CASSIUS] Vexed I am
    Of late with passions of some difference,
    Conceptions only proper to myself,
    Which give some soil, perhaps, to my behaviours;
    But let not therefore my good friends be grieved
    (Among which number, Cassius, be you one)
    Nor construe any further my neglect

Than that poor Brutus, with himself at war,
Forgets the shows of love to other men.
[*Turning to* PORTIA] Good Portia, go to bed.

PORTIA: Is Brutus sick, and is it physical
To walk unbraced and suck up the humors
Of the dank morning?

CASSIUS: Then Brutus, I have much mistook your passion;
By means whereof this breast of mine hath buried
Thoughts of great value ...

PORTIA: What, is Brutus sick,
And will he steal out of his wholesome bed
To dare the vile contagion of the night,
And tempt the rheumy and unpurged air
To add unto his sickness?

CASSIUS: Tell me, good Brutus, can you see your face?

BRUTUS: No, Cassius, for the eye sees not itself
But by reflection, by some other things.

PORTIA: No, my Brutus.
You have some sick offence within your mind
Which by the right and virtue of my place
I ought to know of

CASSIUS: It is very much lamented, Brutus,
That you have no such mirrors as will turn
Your hidden worthiness into your eye,
That you might see your shadow.

PORTIA: Is it expected I should know no secrets
That appertain to you? Am I yourself
But, as it were, in sort or limitation?
To keep with you at meals, comfort your bed,
And talk to you sometimes?

CASSIUS: I have heard
Where many of the best respect in Rome
(Except immortal Caesar) speaking of Brutus,
And groaning underneath this age's yoke
Have wished that noble Brutus had his eyes.

PORTIA: Dwell I but in the suburbs
Of your good pleasure?

CASSIUS: And since you know you cannot see yourself
So well as by reflection, I your glass,
Will modestly discover to yourself
That of yourself which yet you know not of.

PORTIA: If it be no more,
>   Portia is Brutus' harlot, not his wife!

BRUTUS [*Abruptly, reacting to both*]:   Into what dangers would
>   you lead me,
>   That you would have me seek into myself
>   For that which is not in me?

CASSIUS [*Kneeling suddenly to CAESAR – now in Senate scene*]:
>   Pardon Caesar! Caesar, pardon!
>   As low as to thy foot doth Cassius fall
>   To beg enfranchisement of Publius Cimber.

CAESAR: I could be well moved, if I were as you;
>   If I could pray to move, prayers would move me;
>   But I am as constant as the Northern Star,
>   Of whose true-fixed and resting quality
>   There is no fellow in the firmament.
>   The skies are painted with unnumb'red sparks,
>   They are all fire, and every one doth shine;
>   But there's but one in all doth hold his place.

CASSIUS [*From his kneeling position, to BRUTUS*]:   And this man
>   Is now become a god, and Cassius is
>   A wretched creature and must bend his body
>   If Caesar carelessly but nod on him.

CAESAR [*Aside to ANTONY*]:   Let me have men about me that are
>   fat,
>   Sleek-headed men, and such as sleep o' nights.
>   Yon Cassius has a lean and hungry look;
>   He thinks too much, such men are dangerous.

ANTONY: Fear him not, Caesar, he's not dangerous.

CAESAR: Would he were fatter.

ANTONY: He is a noble Roman, and well given.

CASSIUS [*In former scene, to BRUTUS*]:   For once, upon a raw and
>   gusty day,
>   The troubled Tiber chafing at her shores,
>   Caesar said to me ...

CAESAR: He reads much,
>   He is a great observer, and he looks
>   Quite through the deeds of men.

CASSIUS: 'Dar'st thou, Cassius, now
>   Leap in with me into this angry flood
>   And swim to yonder point?'

CAESAR: He loves not plays
>   As thou dost, Antony; he hears no music.

CASSIUS: Upon the word,
    Accoutered as I was, I plunged in
    And bade him follow. So indeed he did.
    But ere we would arrive the point proposed,
    Caesar cried …

CAESAR: Seldom he smiles and smiles in such a sort
    As if he mocked himself and scorned his spirit
    That could be moved to smile at anything.

CASSIUS: 'Help me, Cassius, or I sink!'
    I, as Aeneas, our great ancestor
    Did from the flames of Troy upon his shoulder
    The old Anchieses bear, so from the waves of Tiber
    Did I the tired Caesar!

CAESAR: Such men as he be never at heart's ease
    Whiles they behold a greater than themselves,
    And therefore are they very dangerous.

CASSIUS [*Turning on CAESAR*]: Ye gods, it doth amaze me
    A man of such a feeble temper should
    So get the start of the majestic world
    And bear the palm alone.

CAESAR [*Imperiously, to METELLUS CIMBER*]: I rather tell thee
    what is to be feared
    Than what I fear; for always I am Caesar.
    [*Lamely*] Come on my right hand, for this ear is deaf.

CASSIUS [*Rebelliously*]: Why man, he doth bestride the narrow
    world
    Like a Colossus …

CASCA [*Joining CASSIUS*]: And we petty men
    Walk under his huge legs and peep about
    To find ourselves dishonourable graves.

CASSIUS [*Building in a crescendo*]: I was born as free as
    Caesar …

CASCA: So were you!

CASSIUS: We both have fed as well.

CASCA: And we can both
    Endure the winter's cold as well as he.

CASSIUS: 'Brutus' and 'Casesar'. What should be in that
    'Caesar'?
    Why should that name be sounded more than yours?

CASCA: Write them together –

CASSIUS: Yours is as fair a name.

CASCA: Sound them –

CASSIUS: It doth become the mouth as well.

CASCA: Weigh them –

CASSIUS: It is as heavy. Conjure with 'em.

CASCA: 'Brutus' will start a spirit as soon as 'Caesar'.

CASSIUS: Now in the names of all the gods at once,
Upon what meat doth this our Caesar feed
That he is grown so great?

CAESAR [*Imperiously, in former scene*]: The world – 'tis fur-
nished well with men,
And men are flesh and blood and apprehensive;
Yet in the number I do know but one
That unassailable holds on his rank,
Unshaked of motion, and that I am he!

CALPURNIA [*Cutting into new scene*]: You shall not stir out of
your house today.

CAESAR [*The henpecked husband*]: Caesar shall forth. The
things that threatened me
Ne'er looked but on my back. When they shall see
The face of Caesar, they are vanished.

CALPURNIA: A lioness hath whelped in the streets,
And graves have yawned and yielded up their dead.
Fierce fiery warriors fought upon the clouds
In ranks and squadrons and right form of war,
Which drizzled blood upon the Capitol.
The noise of battle hurtled in the air,
Horses did neigh and dying men did groan,
And ghosts did shriek and squeal about the streets.

CAESAR: Yet Caesar shall go forth, for these predictions
Are to the world in general as to Caesar.

CALPURNIA: When beggars die there are no comets seen;
The heavens themselves blaze forth the death of princes.

CASSIUS [*Enter* CAESAR'S *scene; baitingly*]: Cowards die many
times before their deaths;
The valiant never taste of death but once.

CASCA [*Sardonically*]: Of all the wonders that I yet have heard,
It seems to me most strange that men should fear,
Seeing that death, a necessary end,
Will come when it will come. – What say the augurers?

SOOTHSAYER [*To* CAESAR]: They would not have you to stir
forth today.
Plucking the entrails of an offering forth,
They could not find a heart within the beast.

CASCA: The gods do this in shame of cowardice.
  Caesar should be a beast without a heart
  If he should stay at home today for fear.
CAESAR: No, Caesar shall not. Danger knows full well
  We are two lions littered in one day
  And I the elder and more terrible ...
CASSIUS: Then Caesar shall go forth!
PORTIA [*Entering* CAESAR'S *scene*]:   Do not go forth today. Call
  it my fear
  That keeps you in the house and not your own.
CALPURNIA: We'll send Mark Antony to the Senate House,
  And he shall say you are not well today.
  Let me upon my knee prevail in this.
SOOTHSAYER: They come to fetch thee to the Senate House.
PORTIA: What is't o'clock?
SOOTHSAYER: About the ninth hour, lady.
CALPURNIA: Do not go forth today!
CAESAR [*After a pause*]:   Tell them I will not come today.
CASCA [*Mockingly*]:   'Cannot' is false ...
CASSIUS: ... and that you 'dare not' is falser.
CAESAR: I will not come today. Tell them so.
CASSIUS [*Facetiously*]:   Say he is sick. He had a fever when he
  was in Spain and ...
CASCA [*Mock shocked*]:   Shall Caesar send a lie?
CAESAR: Have I in conquest stretched mine arm so far
  To be feared to tell graybeards the truth?
  Tell them Caesar *will* not come.
SOOTHSAYER: Most mighty Caesar, let me know some cause
  Lest I be laughed at when I tell them so.
CAESAR: The cause is my will: I will not come.
  Calpurnia here, my wife stays me at home.
  She dreamt tonight she saw my statue
  Which, like a fountain with an hundred spouts,
  Did run pure blood and many lusty Romans
  Came smiling and did bathe their hands in it.
SOOTHSAYER: This dream is all amiss interpreted;
  It was a vision fair and fortunate.
CASCA: Your statue spouting blood in many pipes
  In which so many smiling Romans bathed,
  Signifies that ...
SOOTHSAYER: ... from you great Rome shall suck
  Reviving blood ...

CASCA: And that great men shall press
　　For tinctures ...
SOOTHSAYER: stains ...
CASSIUS: relics ...
SOOTHSAYER: and cognizance.
　　This by Calpurnia's dream is signified.
CASCA [*To* SOOTHSAYER, *congratulating him on his improvisation*]:   And this way have you well expounded it!
CASSIUS [*Temptingly*]:   And know, the Senate have concluded
　　To give this day a crown to mighty Caesar.
　　If you shall send them word you will not come,
　　Their minds may change.
CASCA: Besides, it were a mock
　　Apt to be rendered, for someone to say
　　'Break up the Senate till another time,
　　When Caesar's wife shall meet with better dreams.'
CASSIUS: If Caesar hide himself, shall they not whisper
　　'Lo, Caesar is afraid?'
　　Pardon me, Caesar for my dear dear love
　　To your proceeding bids me tell you this,
　　And reason to my love is liable.
CAESAR: How foolish do your fears seem now, Calpurnia!
　　I am ashamed I did yield to them.
　　Give me my robe for I will go.
[BRUTUS *steps behind him, about to place his mantle around* CAESAR'S *shoulders.* FREEZE.]
BRUTUS [*Motionlessly holding mantle around* CAESAR'S *shoulders*]:
　　It must be by his death; and for my part,
　　I know no personal cause to spurn at him,
　　But for the general. He would be crowned.
　　How that might change his nature, there's the question.
　　It is the bright day that brings forth the adder,
　　And that craves wary walking. Crown him that,
　　And then I grant we put a sting in him
　　That at his will he may do danger with.
　　The abuse of greatness is when it disjoins
　　Remorse from power. And to speak truth of Caesar,
　　I have not known when his affections swayed
　　More than his reason. But 'tis a common proof
　　That lowliness is young ambition's ladder,
　　Whereto the climber upward turns his face;
　　But when he once attains the upmost round,

He then unto the ladder turns his back,
Looks in the clouds, scorning the base degrees
By which he did ascend. So Caesar may.
Then lest he may, prevent. And since the quarrel
Will bear no colour for the thing he is,
Fashion it thus: that what he is, augmented,
Would run to these and these extremities;
And therefore think him as a serpent's egg,
Which, hatched, would as his kind grow mischievous,
And kill him in the shell.

CAESAR [*For the first time, acknowledging* BRUTUS'S *presence, turns knowingly to him*]:   Between the acting of a dreadful thing
And the first motion, all the interim is
Like a phantasma or a hideous dream.
The genius and the mortal instruments
Are then in council, and the state of man,
Like to a little kingdom, suffers then
The nature of an insurrection.
[BRUTUS *looks* CAESAR *squarely in the eye, then, as he tries to envelop him in his mantle,* CAESAR *suddenly moves out of it.* CALPURNIA *snatches it from* BRUTUS'S *hands and places it over her husband's shoulders. Both move off, simultaneous with* CASSIUS. CUT INTO THE NEXT SCENE.]

CASSIUS: But what of Cicero? Shall we sound him?

BRUTUS: No, by no means.

METELLUS CIMBER: O, let us have him! for his silver hairs
Will purchase us a good opinion
And buy men's voices to commend our deed.

BRUTUS: O name him not! Let us not break with him,
For he will never follow anything
That other men begin.

CASSIUS: Then leave him out.

CASCA: Indeed, he is not fit.

METELLUS CIMBER: Shall no man else be touched but only Caesar?

CASSIUS: I think it is not meet
Mark Antony, so well beloved of Caesar
Should outlive Caesar. Let Antony and Caesar
Fall together.

ANTONY [*Playing to* BRUTUS *as an augury of things to come*]:   If you have tears, prepare to shed them now.

BRUTUS: Our course will seem too bloody, Caius Cassius,
    To cut the head off and then hack the limbs,
    For Antony is but a limb of Caesar.
ANTONY: You all do know this mantle. I remember
    The first time ever Caesar put it on.
    'Twas on a summer's evening in his tent,
    That day he overcame the Nervii.'
BRUTUS: Let us be sacrificers, but not butchers, Caius.
    Let's kill him boldly –
ANTONY: Look, in this place ran Cassius' dagger through.
BRUTUS: but not wrathfully –
ANTONY: See what a rent the envious Casca made!
BRUTUS: Let's carve him as a dish fit for the gods,
    Now hew him as a carcass fit for hounds.
ANTONY: Through this, the well-loved Brutus stabbed;
    And as he plucked his cursed steel away
    Mark how the blood of Caesar followed it,
    As rushing out of doors to be resolved
    If Brutus so unkindly knocked or no –
BRUTUS: And for Mark Antony, think not of him –
ANTONY: For Brutus, as you know, was Caesar's angel.
    Judge, O you gods, how dearly Caesar loved him!
BRUTUS: For he can do no more than Caesar's arm –
ANTONY: This was the most unkindest cut of all.
BRUTUS: When Casesar's head is off.
CASSIUS: Yet I fear him,
    For the ingrafted love he bears to Caesar...
BRUTUS [*Banishing* ANTONY *from his mind*]:   If he love Caesar,
    all that he can do
    Is to himself – take thought, and die for Caesar.
METELLUS CIMBER: There is no fear in him. Let him not die,
    For he will live and laugh at this hereafter.
    [*THE CLOCK, STRUCK BY AN ACTOR ON THE GONG, SOUNDS THREE.*]
BRUTUS: Peace! count the clock.
CASSIUS: The clock hath stricken three.
CASCA: Tis time to part.
    [*THE CLOCK NOW STRIKES NINE. CUT BACK TO SENATE SCENE*]
METELLUS CIMBER [*Kneeling*]:   Metellus Cimber throws before
    thy seat
    An humble heart.
BRUTUS: [*Kneeling*]:   I kiss thy hand,
  Desiring thee that Publius Cimber may

Have an immediate freedom of repeal.

CASSIUS [*Kneeling*]:   As low as to thy foot doth Cassius fall
To beg enfranchisement of Publius Cimber.

METELLUS CIMBER [*Pleadingly*]:   O Caesar!

CAESAR: Hence! Wilt thou lift up Olympus?

CASSIUS: Great Caesar!

CAESAR: Doth not Brutus bootless kneel.

CASCA: Speak hands for me!

[*All surround CAESAR, now held by PORTIA and CALPURNIA as a sacrifice, and stab him in turn. Then BRUTUS...*]

CAESAR: Et tu, Brute? – Then fall Caesar!

[*As CAESAR falls lifeless, there is a moment's pause. The thunder-sheets are struck by METELLUS CIMBER and the SOOTHSAYER. On the gongs, a slow, dirge-like tattoo. PORTIA and CALPURNIA fill a bowl with CAESAR'S blood, then all quietly file by and wash their hands in it until all are smeared red. This done, a bier appears from upstage and CAESAR is placed upon it. CALPURNIA, helped by PORTIA with ANTONY nearby, apprehensively approaches the bier, looking nervously from side to side. As she stands behind it and looks down at the corpse, all the others turn away.*]

CALPURNIA [*Privately*]:   O, pardon me, thou bleeding piece of earth,
That I am meek and gentle with these butchers!
Thou art the ruins of the noblest man
That ever lived in the tide of times.
Woe to the hand that shed this costly blood!
Over thy wounds now do I prophesy
(Which, like dumb mouths, do ope their ruby lips
To beg the voice and utterance of my tongue),
A curse shall light upon the limbs of men;
Domestic fury and fierce civil strife
Shall cumber all the parts of Italy;
Blood and destruction shall be so in use
And dreadful objects so familiar
That mothers shall but smile when they behold
Their infants quartered with the hands of war,
All pity choked with custom of fell deeds;
And Caesar's spirit, ranging for revenge,
With Ate by his side come hot from hell,
Shall in these confines with a monarch's voice
Cry 'Havoc!' and let slip the dogs of war,

That this foul deed shall smell above the earth
With carrion men, groaning for burial.

[*PORTIA and CALPURNIA move off to one side. Everyone now
assembles behind the bier as for the eulogy. BRUTUS takes up a
position at the head of the bier alongside ANTONY, both looking
down at the corpse. The others surround the bier. BRUTUS
then begins.*]

BRUTUS: Romans, countrymen and lovers, hear me for my
cause and be silent, that you may hear. Believe me for mine
honour, and have respect to mine honour, that you may
believe. Censure me in your wisdom, and awake your senses,
that you may the better judge. If there be any in this
assembly, any dear friend of Caesar's, to him I say that
Brutus' love to Caesar was no less than his. If then that
friend demand why Brutus rose against Caesar, this is my
answer: not that I loved Caesar less, but that I loved Rome
more.

ANTONY: But yesterday the word of Caesar might
Have stood against the world. Now lies he there,
And none so poor to do him reverence.
O masters! If I were disposed to stir
Your hearts and minds to mutiny and rage,
I should do Brutus wrong, and Cassius wrong
Who, you all know, are honourable men.
I will not do them wrong. I rather choose to
Wrong the dead, to wrong myself and you,
Then I will wrong such honourable men.

BRUTUS: Had you rather Caesar were living, and die all slaves,
than that Casesar were dead, to live all freemen? As Caesar
loved me, I weep for him; as he was fortunate, I rejoice at it;
as he was valiant, I honour him – but as he was ambitious, I
slew him.

ANTONY: He hath brought many captives home to Rome,
Whose ransoms did the general coffers fill.
Did this in Caesar seem ambitious?
When that the poor have cried, Caesar hath wept;
Ambition should be made of sterner stuff.

BRUTUS: There is tears for his love; joy for his fortune; honour
for his valour; and death for his ambition.

ANTONY: You all did see that on the Lupercal
I thrice presented him a kingly crown.
Which he did thrice refuse. Was this ambition?

BRUTUS: Who is here so base that would be a bondman? If any speak, for him have I offended.

ANTHONY: You all did love him once, not without cause. What cause witholds you then to mourn for him?

BRUTUS: Who is here so rude that would not be a Roman? If any, speak, for him have I offended.

ANTHONY: O judgement, thou art fled to brutish beasts, And men have lost their reason!

BRUTUS: Who is here so vile that will not love his country? If any, speak, for him have I offended.

ANTONY: Bear with me,
My heart is in the coffin there with Caesar,
And I must pause till it come back to me.

BRUTUS: I pause for a reply.
[*PAUSE as BRUTUS scans the audience for protesters and ANTONY stands, head down, regaining his composure.*]
Then none have I offended. I have done no more to Caesar than you shall do to Brutus. The question of his death is enrolled in the Capitol; his glory not extenuated, wherein he was worthy, nor his offences enforced, for which he suffered death... With this I depart: that, as I slew my best lover for the good of Rome, I have the same dagger for myself when it shall please my country to need my death.
[*BRUTUS steps down from the bier. ANTONY suddenly recovers, and brandishes the will.*]

ANTONY [*As if playing a trump card*]:   Here's a parchment with the seal of Caesar.
I found it in his closet; 'tis his will.
Let but the commons hear this testament
And they would go and kiss dead Caesar's wounds
And dip their napkins in his sacred blood;
Yea beg a hair of him for memory,
And dying, mention it within their wills
Bequeathing it as a rich legacy
Unto their issue.
[*At the sight of the will, CASSIUS, BRUTUS and CASCA turn apprehensively to each other. All the others turn to ANTONY and then back to BRUTUS.*]
To every Roman citizen he gives,
To every several man, seventy-five drachmas.
Moreover he hath left you all his walks,
His private arbours, and new-planted orchards,

On this side Tiber; he hath left them you,
And to your heirs for ever – common pleasures,
To walk abroad and recreate yourselves.
Here was a Caesar! – When comes such another?
[*Havoc. BRUTUS, CASSIUS, CASCA, METELLUS CIMBER and the
other conspirators are shaken by a wave of pandemonium that
breaks through the entire ensemble. The actors pound the
thunder-sheets hanging above. The sound of text formerly played
is heard again – performed simultaneously. The women wail;
the voices of the plebeians are heard roaring; behind this, a
bestial and inhuman voice crying 'Havoc' – as if CALPURNIA'S
prophecy is being fulfilled. Soon, the sound of wild waves
crashing against a rocky shore blankets all other sounds.*

*The PLEBEIANS (played by PINDARUS, VOLUMNIUS, STRATO and
the SOOTHSAYER) suddenly converge. Each has a sheet of parchment
in his hand and as they speak, they each consult their respective lists.*]

FIRST PLEBEIAN [*With list*]:   These many, then, shall die; their
names are pricked.
SECOND PLEBEIAN: Your brother too must die. Consent you to
his death?
FIRST PLEBEIAN: I do consent.
THIRD PLEBEIAN: Prick him down, then.
FIRST PLEBEIAN: Upon condition Publius shall not live
Who is your sister's son.
SECOND PLEBEIAN: He shall not live. Look, with a spot I damn
him.
BRUTUS [*Approaching, unseen*]:   I dreamt tonight that I did
feast with Caesar,
And things unluckily charge my fantasy.
I have no will to wander forth of doors,
Yet something leads me forth.
[*PLEBEIANS, discovering BRUTUS, suddenly apprehend him,
taking hold of him from every side.*]
FIRST PLEBEIAN: What is your name?
SECOND PLEBEIAN: Whither are you going?
THIRD PLEBEIAN: Where do you dwell?
FOURTH PLEBEIAN: Are you a married man or a bachelor?
SECOND PLEBEIAN: Answer every man directly.
FIRST PLEBEIAN: Ay, and briefly.
FOURTH PLEBEIAN: Ay, and wisely.
THIRD PLEBEIAN: Ay, and truly, you were best.

BRUTUS: What is my name? Whither am I going? Where do I dwell? Am I a married man or a bachelor? Then, to answer every man directly and briefly, wisely and truly: wisely I say ... [*looking fearfully to* PORTIA *who nods, indicating he should not admit to her*] I am a bachelor.

SECOND PLEBEIAN: That's as much as to say they are fools that marry. You'll bear me a bang for that, I fear. Proceed – directly.

BRUTUS: Directly, I am going to Caesar's funeral.

FIRST PLEBEIAN: As a friend or an enemy?

BRUTUS: As a friend.

SECOND PLEBEIAN: That matter is answered directly.

FOURTH PLEBEIAN: For your dwelling – briefly.

BRUTUS: Briefly, I dwell by the Capitol.

THIRD PLEBEIAN: Your name, sir. Truly.

BRUTUS: Truly, my name is... [*Looks to* PORTIA, *who again indicates he should not divulge his true identity*] Cinna.

FIRST PLEBEIAN: Tear him to pieces! He's a conspirator.

BRUTUS: I am Cinna the poet! I am Cinna the poet!

FOURTH PLEBEIAN: Tear him for his bad verses! Tear him for his bad verses!

BRUTUS: I am not Cinna the conspirator.

FOURTH PLEBEIAN: It is no matter; his name's Cinna! Pluck but his name out of his heart, and turn him going.

THIRD PLEBEIAN: Tear him, tear him! Come, brands, ho! firebrands!

FIRST PLEBEIAN: Revenge!

SECOND PLEBEIAN: About!

THIRD PLEBEIAN: Seek!

FOURTH PLEBEIAN: Burn!

FIRST PLEBEIAN: Fire!

SECOND PLEBEIAN: Kill!

THIRD PLEBEIAN: Slay!

FOURTH PLEBEIAN: Let not a traitor live!

FIRST PLEBEIAN: We'll burn the house of Brutus!

SECOND PLEBEIAN: Burn all!

THIRD PLEBEIAN: Some to Decius' house...

FOURTH PLEBEIAN: Some to Casca's!

THIRD PLEBEIAN: Some to Ligurius'!

ALL: Away! Go!
    [*CALPURNIUA doles out flaming firebrands to each of the PLEBEIANS. They encircle BRUTUS, brandishing them menacingly*

close to his face, then dash out. CASSIUS opens his eyes, hoping the nightmare is over, and confronts CAESAR full face.]

CAESAR [*With singeing cynicism*]:   How many ages hence
　　Shall this our lofty scene be acted over
　　In states unborn and accents yet unknown.
　　[*All leave as OCTAVIUS CAESAR's servant and MARK ANTONY meet in the centre*]

ANTONY: You serve Octavius Caesar, do you not?

SERVANT: I do, Mark Antony.

ANTONY: Caesar did write for him to come to Rome.

SERVANT: He did receive his letters and is coming
　　He lies tonight within seven leagues of Rome.

ANTONY: Post back with speed and tell him what hath chanced.
　　Here is a mourning Rome, a dangerous Rome,
　　No Rome of safety for Octavius yet.
　　Hie hence and tell him so. [*Messenger goes.*]
　　Now let it work. Mischief, thou art afoot,
　　Take thou what course thou wilt.
　　[*CASCA and METELLUS CIMBER with cloaks, disguised, trying to flee the city. Stopped by taunting PLEBEIANS.*]

FIRST PLEBEIAN: Hence! home, you idle creatures, get you home!
　　Is this a holiday? What, know you not,
　　Being mechanical, you ought not walk
　　Upon a labouring day without the sign
　　Of your profession? Speak, what trade art thou?

METELLUS CIMBER [*In a false voice*]:   Why sir, a carpenter.

SECOND PLEBEIAN: Where is thy leather apron and thy rule?
　　You, sir, what trade are you?

CASCA [*In a false voice*]:   Truly sir, in respect of a fine workman,
　　I am but as you would say, a cobbler.

SECOND PLEBEIAN: But what trade art thou? Answer me directly!

CASCA: A trade sir, that I hope I may use with a safe conscience,
　　which is indeed, a mender of bad soles.

SECOND PLEBEIAN: What trade, thou knave? Thou naughty
　　knave, what trade?

CASCA: Nay, I beseech you, sir, be not out with me. Yet if you
　　be out, sir, I can mend you.

SECOND PLEBEIAN: What mean'st thou by that? Mend me, thou
　　saucy fellow?

CASCA: Why sir, cobble you.

THIRD PLEBEIAN: Thou art a cobbler, art thou?

CASCA: Truly, sir, all that I live by is the awl. I meddle with no tradesman's matters nor women's matters, but with all. I am indeed, sir, a surgeon to old shoes. When they are in danger, I recover them. As proper men as ever trod upon a neat's leather have gone upon my handiwork.

THIRD PLEBEIAN: But wherefore art not in thy shop today? Why dost thou lead this man about the streets?

CASCA: Truly sir, to wear out his shoes, to get myself into more work.

FIRST PLEBEIAN [*Frightening them away*]:   Be gone! Run to your houses. Away!

[*CASCA and METELLUS CIMBER gratefully dash off, as the PLEBEIANS continue combing the street for subversives.*]

[*Servant and ANTONY re-enter.*]

SERVANT: Sir, Octavius is already come to Rome.

ANTONY: Where is he?

SERVANT: He and Lepidus are at Caesar's house.

ANTONY: And thither will I straight to visit him.
He comes upon a wish. Fortune is merry,
And in this mood will give us anything.

SERVANT: I heard him say Brutus and Cassius
Aré rid like madmen through the gates of Rome.

ANTONY: Belike they had some notice of the people,
How I had moved them. Bring me to Octavius.

[*As the conflict between CAESAR's forces and those of BRUTUS and CASSIUS begin to take shape, all the members of the cast play it out on the gongs and thunder-sheets hanging above. They perform the formation of opposing factions, the suspicions of one group against the other, the growing paranoia and distrust ending with the small skirmishes that begin to take place between them. (If desired, mimed actions depicting these actions can be played out in a stylised form in the foreground while the sounds are played out behind.)*

This done, both sides leave the stage which is silent for a moment.

PORTIA enters, moving slowly and lovingly to BRUTUS, who attempts to embrace her, but she sidles away, strangely distracted. BRUTUS moves towards her again, takes her gently by the arms, looks into her eyes, but, as he brings his lips close to hers, she turns away sharply and, just as sharply, BRUTUS cuts into the next scene. PORTIA remains.]

CASSIUS: That you have wrong'd me doth appear in this:
You have condemn'd and noted Lucius Pella
For taking bribes here of the Sardians;
Wherein my letters, praying on his side,
Because I knew the man, were slighted off.

BRUTUS: You wrong'd yourself to write in such a case.

CASSIUS: In such a time as this it is not meet
That every nice offence should bear his comment.

BRUTUS: Let me tell you, Cassius, you yourself
Are much condemn'd to have an itching palm,;
To sell and mart your offices for gold
To undeservers.

CASSIUS: I, an itching palm!
You know that you are Brutus that speak this,
Or by the gods, this speech were else your last.

BRUTUS: The name of Cassius honours this corruption,
And chastisement doth therefore hide his head.

CASSIUS: Chastisement!

BRUTUS: Remember March, the ides of March remember...

PORTIA [*Beside BRUTUS, distractedly affectionate*]:   Dear my lord,
Make me acquainted with your cause of grief.

BRUTUS [*To CASSIUS*]:   Did not great Julius bleed for justice'
sake?
What villain touch'd his body, that did stab,
And not for justice? What! shall one of us,'
That struck the foremost man of all tis world
But for supporting robbers, shall we now
Contaminate our fingers with base bribes,
And sell the mighty space of our large honours,
For so much trash as may be grasped thus?
I had rather be a dog and bay at the moon,
Than such a Roman.

CASSIUS: Brutus, bait not me;
I'll not endure it: you forget yourself,
To hedge me in. I am a soldier, I,
Older in practice, abler than yourself
To make conditions.

BRUTUS: Go to; you are not, Cassius.

CASSIUS: I am.

BRUTUS: I say you are not.

CASSIUS: Urge me no more. I shall forget myself.

BRUTUS: Away, slight man.

CASSIUS: Is't possible?

PORTIA [*Over-affectionately*]: I charm you, by my once com-
mended beauty,
By all your vows of love, and that great vow
Which did incorporate and make us one...

BRUTUS [*Angrily to CASSIUS*]: Must I give way and room to
your rash choler?
Shall I be frighted when a madman stares?

CASSIUS: O ye gods! ye gods! Must I endure this?

BRUTUS: All this! ay, more: fret till your proud heart break;
Go show your slaves how choleric you are,
And make your bondmen tremble. Must I budge?
Must I observe you?
Must I stand and crouch
Under your testy humour? By the gods,
You shall digest the venom of your spleen,
Though it do split you: for, from this day forth,
I'll use you for my mirth, yea, for my laughter,
When you are waspish.

PORTIA: O grant I am a woman, but withal
A woman Lord Brutus took to wife...

CASSIUS: Is it come to this?

BRUTUS: You say you are a better soldier;
Let it appear so; make your vaunting true,
And it shall please me well.

CASSIUS: You wrong me every way: you wrong me Brutus;
I said an elder soldier, not a better;
Did I say 'better'?

BRUTUS: If you did, I care not.

CASSIUS: When Caesar liv'd, he durst not thus have mov'd me.

BRUTUS: Peace, peace. You durst not so have tempted him.

CASSIUS: I durst not!

BRUTUS: No.

CASSIUS: What durst not tempt him!

BRUTUS: For your life you durst not.

CASSIUS: Do not presume too much upon my love;
I may do that I shall be sorry for.

PORTIA [*Gently chiding*]: You have done that you should be
sorry for.

BRUTUS [*Trying to put Portia's memory from him*]: I did send to
you for gold to pay my legions,

Which you denied me: was that done like Cassius?
Should I have answer'd Caius Cassius so?
PORTIA [*Seductively*]:   Y'have ungently Brutus stole from my
    bed.
CASSIUS: I denied you not!
PORTIA: You did.
CASSIUS: I did not; he was but a fool
    That brought my answer back. Brutus hath riv'd my heart.
    A friend should bear his friend's infirmities,
    But Brutus makes mine greater than they are.
BRUTUS: I do not, till you practice them on me.
CASSIUS: You love me not.
PORTIA: I have not from your eyes that gentleness
    And show of love as I was wont to have.
BRUTUS [*To* PORTIA, *gently*]:   You are my true and honourable
    wife,
    As dear to me as the ruddy drops
    That visit my sad heart.
PORTIA: If this be true, then should I know this secret.
BRUTUS [*Sharply, to* CASSIUS]:   I do not like your faults!
CASSIUS: A friendly eye could never see such faults.
BRUTUS: A flatterer's would not, though they do appear
    As huge as high Olympus.
PORTIA: I grant I am a woman, but withal
    A woman that Lord Brutus took to wife.
    I grant I am a woman, but withal
    A woman well-reputed, Cato's daughter.
    Think you I am no stronger than my sex,
    Being so fathered and so husbanded?
CASSIUS: Come, Antony, and young Octavius, come,
    Revenge yourselves alone on Cassius,
    For Cassius is a weary of the world:
    Hated by one he loves; brav'd by his brother;
    Check'd like a bondman; all his faults observ'd,
    Set in a note book, learn'd, and conn'd by rote,
    To cast into my teeth. O! I could weep
    My spirit from mine eyes. There is my dagger,
    And here my naked breast –
PORTIA: I have made strong proof of my constancy,
    Giving myself a voluntary wound
    Here, in the thigh –
CASSIUS: Strike, as thou didst at Caesar; for I know,

When thou didst hate him worst, thou lov'dst him better
Than ever thou lov'dst Cassius.

PORTIA [*Arms around BRUTUS*]:   Can I bear that with patience,
And not my husband's secrets?

BRUTUS [*To PORTIA – lovingly*]:   By and by thy bosom shall partake
The secrets of my heart.
Leave me now with haste.
[*To CASSIUS*] Sheathe your dagger.
O Cassius, you are yoked with a lamb
That carries anger as the flint bears fire,
Who, much enforced, shows a hasty spark,
And straight is cold again.
[*PORTIA moves off from BRUTUS and begins to make a small
fire in the same bowl in which CAESAR's blood was collected.*]

CASSIUS: Hath Cassius liv'd
To be but mirth and laughter to his Brutus,
When grief and blood ill-temper'd vexeth him?

BRUTUS: When I spoke that I was ill-temper'd too.

CASSIUS: Do you confess so much? Give me your hand.

BRUTUS: And my heart too.
[*As BRUTUS clasps CASSIUS to him, PORTIA, having made the
fire in the bowl, swallows it down.*]
[*Confronting PORTIA's memory head-on.*]
O Cassius, I am sick of many griefs.
No man bears sorrow better.
[*PORTIA, facing upstage, still holding the bowl, slumps slowly to
her knees, her head rolling onto her chest.*]
Portia is dead.
[*CASSIUS moves consolingly to BRUTUS as a gong sounds
sepulchrally in the background. PORTIA rises and moves off, as
do CASSIUS and BRUTUS. The gong gives way to a foreboding:
barely audible, the rattle of the thunder-sheet is heard from afar.
This segues into a strict military tattoo on the gongs, as all the
characters create a tight circle, at the centre of which are ANTONY
and OCTAVIUS CAESAR.*]

ANTONY: Brutus and Cassius
Are levying powers. We must straight make head.
Therefore let our alliance be combined,
Our best friends made, and our best means stretched out;
And let us presently go sit in council
How covert matters may be best disclosed
And open perils surest answered.

OCTAVIUS: Let us do so; for we are at the stake
  And bayed about with many enemies;
  And some that smile have in their hearts, I fear,
  Millions of mischiefs.
  [*The circle rotates so that* BRUTUS *and* CASSIUS *are now in centre-position. They break out for their scene and the circle closes behind them.*]
BRUTUS: What do you think
  Of marching to Philippi presently?
CASSIUS: I do not think it good.
  Tis better that the enemy seek us.
  So shall we waste his means, weary his soldiers,
  Doing himself offence, whilst we, lying still,
  Are full of rest, defence, and nimbleness.
BRUTUS: The people twixt Philippi and this ground
  Do stand but in a forced affection,
  For they have grudged us contribution.
  The enemy, marching along by them,
  By them shall make a fuller number up,
  Come on refreshed, new-added and encouraged;
  From which advantage shall we cut him off
  If at Philippi we do face him there,
  These people at our back.
CASSIUS: Hear me, good brother.
BRUTUS: We have tried the utmost of our friends,
  Our legions are brimful, our cause is ripe.
  The enemy increaseth every day;
  We, at the height, are ready to decline.
  There is a tide in the affairs of men
  Which, taken at the flood, leads on to fortune;
  Omitted, all the voyage of their life
  Is bound in shallows and in miseries.
  On such a full sea are we now afloat,
  And we must take the current when it serves
  Or lose our ventures.
CASSIUS: Then with your will, go on.
  We'll along ourselves and meet them at Philippi.
BRUTUS: At Philippi.
  [*They rejoin the circle, which rotates quickly, then breaks formation, leaving* BRUTUS *alone on stage. The thunder-sheets rumble in the background. Behind them, we can make out the sound of the roaring surf and a medley of whispers from the*

•

*other characters. The lights flicker and fade throughout this din,
then return, only to fade once more. Finally, when they come up
for the last time, CAESAR, wearing his bloody mantle, is seated
beside BRUTUS, drinking casually from the same bowl in which
the assassins dipped their hands. PORTIA is at his side, mani-
curing his fingernails; CALPURNIA is bathing his feet.*]

CAESAR [*Whimsically, to BRUTUS, but not looking at him*]:   Are
   you not moved when all the sway of earth
   Shakes like a thing unfirm? O Brutus,
   I have seen tempests when the scolding winds
   Have rived the knotty oaks, and I have seen
   The ambitious ocean swell and rage and foam
   To be exalted with the threat'ning clouds
   But never till tonight, never till now,
   Did I go through a tempest dropping fire:
   Either there is a civil strife in heaven,
   Or else the world, too saucy with the gods,
   Incenses them to send destruction.

BRUTUS [*Calmly, not terrified*]:   I think it is the weakness of mine
   eyes
   That shapes this monstrous apparition.
   Art thou some god, some angel or some devil,
   That mak'st my blood cold and my hair to stare?
   Speak to me what thou art.

CAESAR: A common slave – you know him well by sight –
   Held up his left hand, which did flame and burn
   Like twenty torches joined; and yet his hand,
   Not sensible of fire, remained unscorched.

BRUTUS: Why com'st thou?

CAESAR [*Pushing on, ignoring him*]:   Against the Capitol I met a
   lion,
   Who glared upon me and went surly by
   Without annoying me. And there were drawn
   Upon a heap a hundred ghastly women,
   Transformed with their fear, who swore they saw
   Men, all in fire, walk up and down the streets.
   And yesterday the bird of night did sit
   Even at noonday upon the market place,
   Hooting and shrieking.

BRUTUS: What art thou?

CAESAR: If you would consider the true cause
   Why all these fires, why all these gliding ghosts,

Why birds and beasts, from quality and kind;
Why old men, fools and children calculate;
Why all these things change from their ordinance,
To their natures and preformed faculties,
To monstrous quality, why, you shall find
That heaven hath infused them with these spirits
To make them instruments of fear and warning
Unto some monstrous state.

BRUTUS: Speak to me what thou art?

CAESAR [*Self-evidently, turning to him for the first time*]:   Thy evil spirit, Brutus.

BRUTUS: Why com'st thou?

CAESAR: To tell thee thou shalt see me at Philippi.

BRUTUS: Well: then I shall see thee again?

CAESAR: Ay, at Philippi.

BRUTUS: Why, I will see thee at Philippi then.

CAESAR [*Toodle-oo-ing*]:   At Philippi.

> [*CASSIUS, CASCA and METELLUS CIMBER, sitting, as if around a campfire. As CASCA (who has had too much to drink) speaks, CASSIUS is lost in his own thoughts.*]

CASCA: You know that I held Epicurus strong
And his opinion. Now I change my mind
And partly credit things that do presage.
Coming from Sardis, on our former ensign
Two mighty eagles fell, and there they perched,
Gorging and feeding from our soldier's hands,
Who to Philippi here consorted us.
This morning are they fled away and gone,
And in their steads do ravens, crows, and kites
Fly o'er our heads and downward look on us
As we were sickly prey. Their shadows seem
A canopy most fatal, under which
Our army lies, ready to give up the ghost.

CASSIUS: This is my birthday; as this very day
Was Cassius born. Give me thy hand, Casca
Be thou my witness that against my will
(As Pompey was) am I compelled to set
Upon one battle all our liberties.
> [*Brutus joins the group and sits with the others.*]
Now, most noble Brutus,
The gods today stand friendly, that we may
Lovers in peace, lead on our days to age!

But since the affairs of men rest still uncertain
Let's reason with the worst that may befall.
If we do lose this battle, then is this
The very last time we shall speak together.
What are you then determined to do?

BRUTUS: Even by the rule of that philosophy
By which I did blame Cato for the death
Which he did give himself – I know not how
But I do find it cowardly and vile,
For fear of what might fall, so to prevent
The time of life – arming myself with patience
To stay the providence of some high powers
That govern us below.

CASSIUS: Then if we lose this battle,
You are contented to be led in triumph
Through the streets of Rome.

BRUTUS: No, Cassius, no. Think not, thou noble Roman,
That ever Brutus will go bound to Rome.
He bears too great a mind. But this same day
Must end that work the ides of March begun,
And whether we shall meet again I know not.
Therefore our everlasting farewell take.
For ever and for ever farewell, Cassius!
If not, why then this parting was well made.
[*Takes CASSIUS's hand.*]

CASSIUS: For ever and for ever farewell, Brutus!
If we do meet again, we'll smile indeed;
If not, 'tis true this parting was well made.
[*Takes BRUTUS's hand, then all three take hands.*]

CASCA: O that a man might know
The end of this day's business ere it come!

BRUTUS: But it sufficeth that the day will end,
And then the end is known.
[*The gong, hanging centre, is struck, followed by a series of
consecutive (lesser) gong-strokes. All are alerted into battle
positions. CAESAR moves into the central position and stretches
out his arms, left and right, as if he were the rope in a tug-of-
war. BRUTUS and the conspirators, now joined by VOLUMNIUS,
STRATO, PINDARUS and TITINIUS (formerly the PLEBEIANS)
take hold of one side as OCTAVIUS and ANTONY, joined by four
new followers, take the other. There are equal numbers on each*

side. In the background CALPURNIA *and* PORTIA *accompany the battle action on the gongs.*

Both sides begin pulling strenuously in their own favour.]

BRUTUS: Ride, ride, Messala, ride and give these bills
Unto the legions on the other side.
Let them set on at once, for I perceive
But cold demeanor in Octavius' wing,
And sudden push gives them the overthrow.
Ride, ride, Messala! Let them all come down.
[*Each group – with* CAESAR *still in the middle – exchanges places, still to the accompaniment of the gongs.*]

OCTAVIUS: Now, Antony, our hopes are answered.
You said the enemy would not come down,
But keep the hills and upper regions.
It proves not so, their battles are at hand!

ANTONY: Octavius, lead your battle softly on
Upon the left hand of the even field.

OCTAVIUS: Upon the right hand I. Keep thou the left.

ANTONY: Why do you cross me in this exigent?

OCTAVIUS: I do not cross you; but I will do so.
[*The group, applying new pressure (and again to the accompaniment of the gongs) again exchanges places,* CAESAR *still firm at the centre point. Now,* BRUTUS'S *side loses one or two of its followers.*]

CASSIUS: O look, Titinius, look! The villains fly!
Myself have to mine own turned enemy.

TITINIUS: O Cassius, Brutus gave the word too early,
Who, having some advantage on Octavius
Took it too eagerly. His soldiers fell to spoil,
Whilst we by Antony are all enclosed.

CASCA: Fly further off, my lord! fly further off!
Mark Antony is in your tents, my lord.
Fly therefore, noble Cassius, fly far off!
[*The group again changes position;* CAESAR *still the centre point.*]

OCTAVIUS: I was not born to die on Brutus' sword!
Defiance, traitors, hurl we in your teeth!

CASSIUS: Why, now blow wind, swell billow, and swim bark!
The storm is up, and all is on the hazard.
[*They make a renewed assault.*]

OCTAVIUS: Come Antony, away!
[*The group shifts position again.*]

CASCA: Titinius is enclosed round about
   With horsemen that make to him on the spur.
   Yet he spurs on. Now they are almost on him.
   [*OCTAVIUS's group shouts victoriously.*]
   He's ta'en! And hark!
   They shout for joy.
BRUTUS: Yet countrymen, O yet hold up your heads!
   What bastard doth not? Who will go with me?
   I will proclaim my name about the field.
   I am Brutus. Marcus Brutus, I!
   Brutus, my country's friend. Know me for Brutus!
   [*There is one final push from OCTAVIUS's side. CAESAR lets fall
   BRUTUS's faction and they scatter away.*]
OCTAVIUS'S GROUP: Brutus is ta'en! Brutus is ta'en!
   [*The group, now in a wide semi-circle, surrounds BRUTUS and
   CASSIUS, who stand in their midst. CASSIUS kneels down beside
   PINDARUS, one of his soldiers in the group.*]
CASSIUS: Come hither sirrah.
   In Parthia did I take thee prisoner,
   And then I swore thee, saving of thy life,
   That whatsoever I did bid thee do,
   Thou shouldst attempt it. Come now, keep thine oath.
   Now be a freeman, and with this good sword,
   That ran through Caesar's bowels, search this bosom.
   Stand not to answer. Here, take thou the hilts,
   And when my face is covered...
   [*CAESAR covers his eyes with his hand.*]
   as t'is now,
   Guide thou the sword.
   [*PINDARUS looks to CAESAR, then poises the sword before
   CASSIUS; CAESAR takes PINDARUS's hand and guides the point
   slowly into CASSIUS's heart.*]
   Caesar, thou art revenged
   Even with the sword that killed thee.
   [*PINDARUS removes the body of CASSIUS. BRUTUS, sword in
   hand, approaches other persons in the semi-circle. As he moves
   pleadingly to each one, they turn their back on him. Finally, he
   approaches VOLUMNIUS.*]
BRUTUS: The ghost of Caesar hath appeared to me
   Two several times by night – at Sardis once,
   And this last night here in Philippi fields.
   I know my hour is come.

169

VOLUMNIUS: Not so, my lord.

BRUTUS: Nay, I am sure it is, Volumnius.
   Thou seest the world, Volumnius, how it goes.
   Our enemies have beat us to the pit.
   It is more worthy to leap in ourselves
   Than tarry till they push us. Good Volumnius,
   Thou know'st that we two went to school together.
   Even for that our love of old, I prithee
   Hold thou my sword's hilt whilst I run on it.

VOLUMNIUS: That's not an office for a friend, my lord.
   [*Steps back into the semi-circle and turns his back on* BRUTUS,
   *who continues to move towards others, all of whom turn their
   back on him as soon as he approaches. Until he gets to* STRATO,
   who is too frightened to turn away.]

BRUTUS: I prithee Strato, stay thou by thy lord.
   Thou art a fellow of good respect;
   Thy life hath had some snatch of honour in it.
   Hold then my sword, and turn away thy face
   While I do run upon it. Wilt thou, Strato?
   [*Gives him his sword.*]
   [STRATO *looks reluctantly from side to side.* PORTIA *comes
   forward, takes his place and holds the sword in place as* BRUTUS
   runs on it. As he falls, CAESAR *steps forward and catches the
   dying man in his arms.*]
   I shall have glory by this losing day
   More than Octavius and Mark Antony
   By this vile conquest shall attain unto.
   So fare you well at once, for Brutus' tongue
   Hath almost ended his life's history.
   Night hangs upon mine eyes; my bones would rest,
   That have but laboured to attain this hour.
   [*He dies.*]

PORTIA [*Tenderly, taking the body from Caesar*]:   His life was
   gentle, and the elements
   So mixed in him that Nature might stand up
   And say to all the world, 'This was a man!'
   [*The group lifts* BRUTUS *and ceremonially carries him out,
   leaving* CAESAR *alone on stage.*
   CAESAR *looks up to the thunder-sheets, gongs and bells, then
   slowly raises his hand as a signal. The thunder-sheets, gongs
   and bells are very slowly flown up into the flies. As he walks off,
   a young, contemporary schoolboy – maybe twelve or thirteen –*

enters, holding a copy of JULIUS CAESAR *and trying to commit a speech to memory. He speaks haltingly and reads the verse awkwardly without conveying any of its true significance.*]

SCHOOLBOY [*Engrossed in book*]:   'Wherefore rejoice? What conquests brings he home?

What tribu ... tribu ... tribu-taries follow him to Rome...

To grace in captive bonds – *bonds!* – his chariot wheels?

You blocks-you stones-you-'

[*Senses he is hurrying, slows up.*]

You Blocks – You Stones – You worse Than Senseless Things

Knew you not ... Pom ... knew you not – Pompee? – Pompey?'

[LIGHTS BEGIN TO FADE]

Many a time and oft

Have you climbed up to walls – and battlements

[*Repeating methodically, under his breath*] walls-and-battlements...

To – tow'rs and – windows, – yea, to chimney-tops –

Your infants in your arms, and there have sat

The livelong day, with patient ex-pec-ta-tion

To see great Pompee [*corrects himself*] Pompey pass the streets of Rome.'

[THE LIGHTS ARE OUT]

Index